Poverty
is NOT a
Learning Disability

Poverty is NOT a Learning Disability

Equalizing Opportunities for Low SES Students

Tish Howard
Sandy Grogan Dresser
With **Dennis R. Dunklee**

CORWIN
A SAGE Company

For information:

Corwin
A SAGE Company
2455 Teller Road
Thousand Oaks, California 91320
(800) 233-9936
Fax: (800) 417-2466
www.corwinpress.com

SAGE India Pvt. Ltd.
B 1/I 1 Mohan Cooperative
   Industrial Area
Mathura Road, New Delhi 110 044
India

SAGE Ltd.
1 Oliver's Yard
55 City Road
London EC1Y 1SP
United Kingdom

SAGE Asia-Pacific Pte. Ltd.
33 Pekin Street #02-01
Far East Square
Singapore 048763

Printed in the United States of America.

Library of Congress Cataloging-in-Publication Data

Howard, Tish.
Poverty is not a learning disability: equalizing opportunities for low SES children / Tish Howard and Sandy Grogan Dresser; with Dennis R. Dunklee.
      p. cm.
Includes bibliographical references.
ISBN 978-1-4129-6903-1 (cloth)
ISBN 978-1-4129-6904-8 (pbk.)

   1. Children with social disabilities—Education (Elementary)—United States. 2. Poor children—Education (Elementary)—United States. 3. Readiness for school—United States. 4. Educational equalization—United States. I. Dresser, Sandy Grogan. II. Dunklee, Dennis R. III. Title.

LC4069.3.H69 2009
372.18′26942—dc22   2009011180

This book is printed on acid-free paper.

11   12   13   14   15   10 9   8   7   6   5   4   3

Acquisitions Editor:	Arnis Burvikovs
Associate Editor:	Desirée A. Bartlett
Production Editor:	Jane Haenel
Copy Editor:	Adam Dunham
Typesetter:	C&M Digitals (P) Ltd.
Proofreader:	Gail Fay
Cover and Graphic Designer:	Michael Dubowe

Contents

Preface

From the time the Soviet Union launched Sputnik in 1957, through the publication in 1983 of the *A Nation at Risk* report by the National Commission on Excellence in Education, and since the enactment of the No Child Left Behind Act in 2001, we've been told—and shown statistics to prove—that our public schools are failing to teach our children to read, write, and do basic mathematics, let alone keep up with the education successes of other industrialized countries. At least since the 1980s, the focus of criticism has been on inner-city or urban schools where student standardized test scores have most consistently been low. These are schools that serve a high number of students who come from poverty- or near-poverty-level homes, a high percentage of whom are also from minority or recent immigrant cultures. The unfortunate, but almost inevitable, conclusion that our nation's print and broadcast media have drawn from this situation is that children of poverty are somehow unable to learn as effectively as their middle- and upper-class peers. While the authors of this book can't argue with the reported standardized test scores, we adamantly disagree with the conclusion. We don't believe that poverty makes children unable, or even unwilling, to learn.

The statistics that compelled us to take a stand on the education of children of poverty are those that report the incredibly high percentage of children of poverty, which we define as children from low socioeconomic environments, who are annually referred for special education identification as learning disabled (LD)—a symptom, we believe, of a perception in the minds of educators that poverty is a learning disability. Our years of experience in the field of education led us to believe that the problems low socioeconomic status (low SES) students experience in school are not based on identifiable learning disabilities but rather on the lack of readiness skills needed to be successful in schools that assume all students come to school equally prepared to learn and educators' inability to recognize and mitigate this lack.

This book is based on the findings of a 2006 study (Howard, 2007) of teachers and principals of low SES students who have successfully, and over an extended period of time, provided equal education opportunities to low SES children and brought them into the successful mainstream of students, without resorting to special education identification. In it, we present strategies and techniques the exemplary teachers and principals we observed use to humanize the school and classroom environments and make it possible for their low SES, minority, and multicultural students to overcome the challenges of poverty, cultural differences, and school readiness and succeed academically on a par with their more economically advantaged peers. In addition to identifying the successful pedagogical and school leadership strategies and techniques we observed, we offer proven management strategies to facilitate implementation of the changes we recommend in the way schools that serve low SES children operate.

As the authors of this book, we combined our more than 75 years of experience in the field of education, as teachers, principals, central office administrators, and university professors, with many years of experience in the fields of human resources and organizational management to present a comprehensive look at the problem and its solutions. Although the focus of this book is the overwhelming misidentification of low SES children as LD, we believe that the education and management strategies and techniques we present are applicable to the education enterprise as a whole and will be valuable to educators everywhere.

Acknowledgments

Corwin gratefully acknowledges the contributions of the following individuals:

Elizabeth Alvarez, Assistant Principal
John C. Dore Elementary School
Chicago, IL

Rebecca S. Compton, Professor
Elementary Education
East Central University
Ada, OK

Mary Beth Cunat, Director, Principal Professional Development
Chicago Public Schools
Chicago, IL

Daniel C. Elliott, Professor and Curriculum Specialist
Center for Online Learning and Technology
Azusa Pacific University
Azusa, CA

Jim Hoogheem, Retired Principal
Fernbrook Elementary School
Maple Grove, MN

Kevin Olds, Principal
Estacada Junior High School
Estacada, OR

About the Authors

 **Tish Howard** has 20 years of experience as an educator working with children and parents in low SES schools. She is an elementary principal in a Title I school in which 43% of its families are classified as living in poverty. In this position, Dr. Howard is responsible for the design and implementation of numerous programs and a school climate that raised the level of student academic success and closed the achievement gap between students of poverty and those residing in homes of economic stability. Dr. Howard works with parents, civic associations, clergy, and the business community to level the economic playing field for disadvantaged students and has implemented numerous initiatives to provide the necessary background knowledge many children from poverty lack when entering school.

Prior to her role as a school administrator, Dr. Howard served 10 years as a speech and language pathologist with a full caseload of language delayed children. She spent 8 of those 10 years delivering services to emotionally disturbed adolescent males in an alternative educational setting. It was in that capacity that Dr. Howard introduced inclusion language therapy to her school district, as opposed to the standard pull out method. This form of therapeutic delivery is now widely used districtwide.

Dr. Howard has served as an education consultant for local preschool and summer camp experiences. She designed an educational summer experience for low SES children that focused on providing a foundation for the academic challenges they would face in the upcoming academic year. She also served on the Minority Student Achievement Board for her school system and has presented programs on intervention methods at the local school and university level.

Dr. Howard earned her bachelor's and master's degrees in speech and language pathology from Indiana University of Pennsylvania and her PhD in education leadership from George Mason University. While completing her postgraduate work, Dr. Howard was a contributing writer to the *USA Today* educational website, and she continues to mentor prospective administrators through the university mentoring program. She has been nominated for Principal of the Year honors in her school district, recognized by the Association of Supervision and Curriculum Development for development of positive school climate, and featured in numerous television and print articles.

Sandy Grogan Dresser is a human resources management consultant who consults with clients in the areas of compensation, performance management, management development, employee communications, and human resources policy and administration. She has more than 30 years experience in the field of human resources management, including 6 years in her private consulting practice and 15 years as an assistant vice president with Aon Consulting in Bethesda, Maryland. Prior to joining Aon, Ms. Dresser served as a human resources director in both the public and private not-for-profit sectors. She has also served as an executive development consultant to a number of federal departments and agencies.

Ms. Dresser served 12 years as a public school teacher and administrator, during which time she was instrumental in the development and implementation of significant educational change in the implementation of middle schools and managed the human resources function of a metropolitan school district. In addition to standard personnel administration, she was responsible for coordinating a reorganization plan that included the closing of nine junior high schools, the opening of six new middle schools, and the reassignment of 300 employees. In this role, she devised and directed a staff reassignment procedure that effected minimum disruption and a high level of satisfaction among teachers, administrators, students, and parents.

A graduate of the University of North Carolina and Kansas University, Ms. Dresser holds bachelor's degrees in history and education and a master's degree in education policy and administration. She is the author of numerous articles published in professional journals, and she frequently presents seminars for professional associations on topics in the human resources management field.

Dennis R. Dunklee is professor emeritus in the Education Leadership Department in the Graduate School of Education at George Mason University. During his 25 years in public schools, he served as a teacher, elementary school principal, junior high and middle school principal, high school principal, and central office administrator. During his tenure as a professor, he taught courses in education law and school leadership and served as an advisor and chair for masters in school administration candidates. He continues to advise doctoral candidates in school leadership and serves as an adjunct professor. Because of his expertise and practical experience, he is frequently called on to consult in the areas of effective schools, school law, administrator evaluation, instructional supervision, school-community relations, problem solving, and conflict resolution. In addition, he has been involved as a consultant and expert witness in numerous school-related lawsuits nationwide. As a university scholar and researcher, he published 10 textbooks, 2 monographs, and more than 100 articles on issues in the fields of school law, business management, administrative practice, and leadership theory. He is active in a number of professional organizations; has presented papers at international, national, regional, state, and local conferences; and is a widely sought-after clinician for inservice workshops. Dr. Dunklee was an invited participant and presenter in the 2005 Oxford (University) Round Table on Education Law: Individual Rights and Freedoms, and in 2007, he was recognized by Kappa Delta Pi as an educator "who exemplifies the high professional, intellectual, and personal standards our society promotes, who demonstrates dedication to educators, students, and the field of education."

Dr. Dunklee has written or cowritten seven books for Corwin. His other Corwin books are *You Sound Taller on the Telephone: A Practitioner's View of the Principalship* (1999), *If You Want to Lead Not Just Manage* (2000), *The Principal's Quick Reference Guide to School Law* (with Robert J. Shoop, 2002), *Strategic Listening for School Leaders* (with Jeannine Tate, 2005), *Anatomy of a Lawsuit: What Every Education Leader Should Know About Legal Actions* (with Robert J. Shoop, 2006), and *The Principal's Quick Reference Guide to School Law,* 2nd edition (with Robert J. Shoop, 2006).

He received his PhD in school administration and foundations from Kansas State University. His major area of research was in the field of education law, and his dissertation was on tort liability for negligence. He holds a master's degree in elementary and secondary school administration from Washburn University.

"Whose child is this?" I asked one day
Seeing a little one out at play
"Mine," said the parent with a tender smile
"Mine to keep a little while
To bathe his hands and comb his hair
To tell him what he is to wear
To prepare him that he may always be good
And each day do the things he should."

"Whose child is this?" I asked again
As the door opened and someone came in
"Mine," said the teacher with the same tender smile
"Mine, to keep just for a little while
To teach him how to be gentle and kind
To train and direct his dear little mind
To help him live by every rule
And get the best he can from school."

"Whose child is this?" I ask once more
Just as the little one entered the door
"Ours," said the parent and the teacher as they smiled
And each took the hand of the little child
"Ours to love and train together."

—Anonymous

This book is dedicated to all the hopeful children waiting
for us to discover their possibilities.

Introduction

More than ever, in today's climate of heightened expectations for our nation's schools, principals are in the hot seat to improve teaching and learning. This is a book written primarily for school leaders, specifically school-based administrators, by three authors who currently are, or have been, in the proverbial hot seat for many years. However, by the very nature of its contents, this book has important implications for vice principals, preservice principal candidates, special education specialists, school counselors, and classroom teachers. The book is designed to improve the education of elementary school children of low socioeconomic status (low SES children)—who far too often come to school with low school-readiness skills—by preventing their misidentification as learning disabled (LD).

When educators don't clearly understand the criteria for identification of learning disabilities, don't recognize the difference between learning disabilities and low achievement, nor employ the resources available to assist low achievers, the possibility of elementary school children being misidentified as LD is more likely. This not only places children in special education settings unnecessarily but also prevents timely intervention to what may be the root cause of the poor performance, which, simply stated, is poor school readiness.

The Child Trends Data Bank (2007) reported that, in 2004, the average per student cost was $7,552, and the average cost for special education was an additional $9,369 per student, or $16,921. That means that in 2004 it cost more than twice as much to educate a special education student as it did a regular student. Greene and Winters (2007) noted that, from 1977 through 2003, spending on special education services almost doubled due to the fact that the number of students served by special education increased by 76%. With LD placements increasing from 796,000 in 1977 to nearly 3 million in 2003, LD represented a particularly costly segment of the special education budget. A recent report published by IDEA Data shows that from 2001 through 2005 nearly half of all special education placements were in LD. In 2005, 2,780,218 students (ages 6–21), or 45% of all special education students, received LD services. According to IDEA Data, the cost that year to educate 5.2% of the total student population equaled 11% of the total education budget (U.S. Department of Education, 2008).

Between 1997 and 2004, a consistently higher percentage of children diagnosed as LD came from low SES households (Child Trends Data Bank, 2007). It's possible that the increase in the percentage of low SES students identified as LD is because their behaviors, learning styles, and attending patterns—which differ from those exhibited by middle- and upper-class White students—influence their inappropriate referral to special education. In some cases, differences in these behaviors may be misinterpreted as a learning disability rather than cultural and learning differences.

This book for school leaders is designed to improve the education of low SES elementary school children with low school-readiness skills by identifying workable strategies leaders can use to prevent these students' misidentification as LD. It's built on the premise that the time and money spent on special education services will be better used if we focus on the needs of children with low school-readiness skills before their deficits become so great that neither intervention nor remediation will work, and the children's self-perceptions are so badly damaged that they quit trying to succeed and accept failure. It does so by sharing practical research from classrooms and schools that are meeting the varying developmental and environmental needs of low SES students. The book takes an in-depth look at schools that have realized effective turnarounds in remarkable time frames, resulting in increased academic performance, community support, business partnerships, and significant decreases in student behaviors that distract from academic success. It includes specific examples of the successful implementation of strategies that work in real classrooms, schools, and communities.

This book is about optimism as a central tenet of elementary schools' day-to-day teaching/learning programs and school-community relationships. We, the authors, believe that optimism is strongly connected to hope for the future and crucial to providing children with a positive vision of their future. Unfortunately, many (parents, teachers, students, and school administrators) in today's school communities have a tremendous capacity for creative pessimism. They don't expect success for low SES children—that is, they exhibit "deficit perception" regarding such children. And because children inevitably endeavor to fit our words, actions, and deeds into narratives of their own, it's essential that we, the education community, ensure that we're not providing them with a view of their futures that corrodes hope, produces undue fear, and denigrates the value of the only reality they have.

This book is also about how to build trusting relationships throughout the school community—among teachers, students, administrators, the school staff, and parents. A school community should never be mired in pessimism but move continuously forward in a process of engaging in reform to ensure the academic achievement of students. We believe that school reform, including the building of trusting relationships, is about more than just choosing a model. It's about people making real changes and being able to trust each other to follow through on these changes.

More important, this book looks at the role that administrators' and teachers' deficit perception plays in the overall teaching/learning dynamic when working with low SES children who have low school-readiness skills. This book answers critical questions about how to turn a school into an integrated school-community organization in which optimism and positive relationships are the focal point of the day-to-day teaching/learning environment—that is, how school administrators and teachers identify the learning needs of children with low school-readiness skills and how school administrators and teachers work cooperatively with parents to prepare children with low school-readiness skills to meet grade-level expectations while avoiding special education or retention.

In addition to identifying educational and administrative strategies for working with low SES children, this book goes a step further and addresses the change management, staff selection, and performance management strategies necessary to the effective implementation of the needed educational strategies. The goal of this book is to present practitioners with workable strategies that are practical, low cost, and immediately applicable to the school environment.

1

The Changing Realities of America's Public Education

Foundational Facts and Implications

The face of education is changing. As any of us who have taught or served as administrators in a public school system for 10 years or more can tell you, these changes translate into challenges we face each day. The demographic changes and educational effects of persistent poverty are foreign to many of us who look into the expectant and hopeful eyes of today's students and find ourselves at a loss as to where to start. This chapter provides a foundation for the ideas and education strategies presented in the rest of this book.

DIVERSITY

While the enrollment in public schools between 2000 and 2009 has remained generally stable, other statistics surrounding public school education have transformed the daily operations of schools. One of the most visible changes is the growing diversity in our schools. Blacks, Hispanics, and children from a wide array of Asian and Middle Eastern cultures now make up nearly half of students nationwide and are the dominant majorities in many of the schools in low-income (low SES) neighborhoods.

While the growing diversity is celebrated in many of our nation's public schools, the reality of an increasingly large number of second-language learners poses increasing challenges. Students who speak English as a second language (ESL) make up a significant percentage of our nation's school population. Schools currently provide programs for nearly 3 million ESL students, and it's estimated that this population is growing two and a half times faster than that of native English speaking students (Shore, 2005). Those of us who work in low SES schools know that the tasks that face our teachers include teaching ESL students academic skills, supporting their English proficiency, helping them adjust to the school setting, and fostering their adaptation to the American culture. We and our teachers must also develop avenues for communicating with the parents of ESL students. Quite frequently, such communication requires translators and involves scheduling conflicts around parents who often have more than one job.

POVERTY

Another challenge we face is the growing number of students who live at or below the poverty line. Recent statistics reveal that an additional 1.3 million children fell into poverty between 2000 and 2005, the most recent dates for which data is available. In fact, a child's likelihood of being poor has increased by almost 9% (Children's Defense Fund, 2006). In more concrete terms, one out of every six children is poor, and one in every three Black children lives in poverty.

Of special interest to us is the clustering of poor minorities in neighborhood schools. The poverty divide is double edged for minority students. Not only are Black, Hispanic, and children of recent immigrants more likely to live in poor families, they are also more likely to live in impoverished neighborhoods. While we tend to assume that all poor children live in neighborhoods that are poor, that's often not the case with poor White children. Research actually shows that in our largest metropolitan areas very few White low SES children (4%) live in poor neighborhoods, while nearly half of Asian low SES children and the vast majority of Black and Hispanic low SES children do (Harvard Public Health, 2007). White low SES students appear to be dispersed among more affluent peers. The problem for those of us who work in schools in low SES neighborhoods is that the majority of the students often lack the educational resources that promote learning enjoyed by children from higher-income homes, including parent involvement, books, educational experiences, and access to and comfort with technology, to name just a few.

SCHOOL READINESS

Most of us would agree that the knowledge and skills that children have in place when they begin school are likely the result of their experiences prior to school. For many children, the most influential learning ground prior to the schoolhouse is the home. Past research has established that individual differences in the experiences of children can be extremely predictive in the cognitive development level achieved (Bradley & Corwyn, 1999). The National Education Goals Panel (1997) subgroup delineated five specific areas that signal school readiness for children:

1. *Physical well-being and development*, including good nutrition; immunizations; physical skills and gross motor abilities, such as running and jumping; and fine motor skills, such as using crayons and puzzles.

2. *Social and emotional development*, specifically a sense of confidence that allows children to fully participate in a classroom, experience with turn taking, following directions, working alone and as a group member, and the ability to form friendships.

3. *Supportive environments* provided by the adults in a child's life that foster learning and promote curiosity, creativity, motivation, independence, cooperation, and persistence so children can meet new challenges.

4. *Language usage*, including talking, listening, scribbling, and composing. Children who use language appropriately generally have been read to and encouraged to communicate their thoughts, feelings, and experiences.

5. *Cognition and knowledge*, including being familiar and comfortable with basic knowledge such as patterns, relationships, cause and effect, and problem solving.

Poverty appears to be the leading risk factor and barrier to ensuring that the five areas of development and growth identified above are intact.

Poor children typically enter school a full year and a half behind their middle-class peers in language ability, studies show. So, millions of kids start their lives with an educational deficit. That's why we have to get to them while they are still tots. (Grundel, Oliveira, & Geballe, 2003, p. 5)

While not all children who live in poverty will have a difficult time learning, children who are underdeveloped in one or more of these readiness areas will have a greater chance of experiencing lower achievement than children with all areas intact, and they may very well become candidates for misguided referrals for placement as learning disabled.

The school readiness of children living in poverty may be seriously affected by their economic circumstances. As we know, truly rich school readiness requires access to opportunities that expose children to educational resources and provide them with nurturing experiences and relationships. Unfortunately, many children live in a low socioeconomic environment that, while rich in culture, may not provide the experiences needed to give them the foundations required for academic success. Children develop and learn at optimal levels when they're part of an environment in which they're safe and valued, where their physical well-being is tended to and they feel psychologically secure (National Association for the Education of Young Children, 2004). Such an environment is too often unattainable in low-income neighborhoods.

Research shows that one in three children enters kindergarten not ready for school and that, by the time they begin formal schooling, children in low-income families already lag behind their more affluent peers academically, socially, and physically (Feldman, 2001; Foster, 2000; Gershoff, 2003). A comparison (Lee & Burkham, 2002) of the environment of kindergarteners from the top five richest communities in the nation and those from the five poorest revealed that the children from the poorest communities

- owned just 38 books as compared to 150 in the top fifth;
- were read to much less often—63% of low SES children versus 93% of their more affluent counterparts were read to three or more times per week;
- spent 18 or more hours per week watching television versus 11 or fewer hours from the wealthier homes;
- had moved more—48% had moved at least three times before kindergarten; and
- were much less likely to have seen a play or participate in dance, art, music, or crafts classes.

It's not that the poorest children are incapable of school learning; in most cases they just haven't been exposed to the kinds of experiences that produce learning readiness. Children's genetic predispositions influence their attention, actions, and the responses they have to their environments. However, the opportunities available in children's various environments inevitably influence whether their inherent predispositions are realized. Naturally inquisitive children who grow up in environments that don't provide sufficient opportunities for exploration and discovery may have little opportunity to exercise their natural curiosity. During the time low-income students spend outside of school, they often find themselves in a culture that doesn't provide the kinds of stimulation that support and extend school learning (Feldman, 2001). Research indicates that close to 40% of the associations between economic disadvantage and young children's lower academic performance are directly related to the poorer quality of home learning environments (Smith, Brooks-Gunn, & Klebanov, 1997). It seems clear that children's early childhood experiences play a formative role in their school readiness and account for many of the skill gaps that low-income children demonstrate when they enter public schools (Shonkoff & Phillips, 2000).

We all know that school readiness expectations have been elevated dramatically since the No Child Left Behind (NCLB) Act of 2001 became law. Before NCLB, kindergarteners were expected to learn social skills, tie their shoes, and learn their colors, shapes, and some letters and numbers. Now it's expected they'll *enter* kindergarten with these skills in place and rapidly build on them, and children who haven't mastered basic language, reading, and math skills enter school with barriers to their learning. The U.S. Department of Education's National Center for Education Statistics (2005) cites the three most limiting environmental factors to children's readiness as (1) limited economic resources, (2) parents with low levels of education, and (3) single parenthood. Children's genetic makeup can influence the way they attend, act, and respond to their environment. However, if a child starts school intact and healthy, but the home environment provides few opportunities to stimulate the psychological, social, and emotional abilities required for school success, readiness is significantly impacted and again, too often leads to a learning disabled (LD) referral.

LACK OF PARENT INVOLVEMENT

In today's economy, poor and working-class parents are more likely to work multiple low-wage service-sector jobs, and many of them find themselves ill equipped to navigate the ever-rising expectations of an increasingly competitive educational system (Van Galen, 2007). While low SES doesn't naturally equate to a lack of parents' concern or efforts to ensure a healthy environment for their children, the lack of parental supervision resulting from long work hours often reduces low SES children's opportunity for learning experiences at home.

Even though parents of low SES children rate the importance of education as a route to economic and social mobility highly, their actual involvement in the school community often falls short of the schools' expectations (Casanova, 1996). An ethnographic study by Lareau (1994) illustrated the phenomenon. Lareau compared two first-grade classrooms—one located in a low-income neighborhood and one in a middle-class community. Teachers in both schools expressed the same level of expectation for parent participation. Parents in the low-income neighborhoods were less familiar with the school's curriculum, engaged less in teaching at home, and were less likely to attend school functions. The study found that the lack of participation wasn't necessarily due to lack of concern or commitment; poorer parents just had less time and flexibility to meet parent involvement commitments. Comments from parents also indicated that they lacked confidence in their ability to deal with matters of their children's education and would rather defer to the teachers.

A two-year longitudinal study (Pelletier, 2005) that capitalized on and contributed to a pilot initiative in one school examined the effects of an innovative classroom-based preschool program for four-year-olds and their families on school readiness. The theory behind this program emphasized the ecology of family-school partnerships and relationships in helping children make transitions to school. One significant outcome of the pilot was the differences in teachers' and parents' perceptions of school readiness. In some cases, parents were, again, just too busy with multiple jobs and life's struggles to reflect seriously on the school readiness factors that are of concern to teachers.

DEFICIT PERCEPTIONS

Many teachers don't understand the effects of poverty on school readiness and, as a result, accept the inevitability of impending failure for children of poverty—these teachers exhibit deficit perception. For example, research (O'Hara, 2006) showed that by age three, children whose parents were professionals had vocabularies of about 1,100 words, and children whose parents were on welfare had vocabularies of about 525 words. The children's IQs correlated closely to their vocabularies. The average IQ among the professional children was 117, while the welfare children's IQ averaged 79. Teachers who face classrooms in which the majority of the children arrived unprepared to meet typical school expectations have a formidable task if they try to teach these children the way they've always taught in the past.

If you're an elementary school principal or teacher, you know that it's impossible to start a school year at the same starting point every year. You can't plan a reasonable timeline until you've assessed the readiness levels of the children who come to you in September. If you don't understand the experiences the children bring to school and simply expect that all of them can or will abandon their cultural connections and conform to a school design that's abysmally foreign to them, you'll experience a serious disconnect. The standard of contextualization recommends that teaching and curriculum be connected to the experiences, values, knowledge, and needs of students (C.A.R.E. Advisory, 2003). Unfortunately, teachers too often don't sufficiently understand the children's cultures and environments to make the necessary connections. The majority of educators today are White and have middle-class experiences, and the manner in which they deal with children who aren't ready for school—either by minimizing the barriers or mentally dismissing the children—can seriously impact their students' education futures.

When children's experiences don't match their expectations, too many teachers tend to attribute school problems to "deficient" environments and lower their expectations for the children's success. As educators, we need to be aware of the learning opportunities that may *not* be present in economically disadvantaged homes and consider opportunities to put intervention programs in place rather than "dummy down" the curriculum to insure low SES students' success or assume the children must have a learning disability.

SPECIAL EDUCATION AND NCLB

There's another statistic that has risen consistently in recent years: the identification of children as LD. Since 1976, children identified as specific learning disabled has grown threefold from 2% to 6% of all school-age children. The increase in LD identification far surpasses that of any other disability, including speech and language, emotional disturbance, and mental retardation. The numbers are particularly distressing when disaggregated by poverty. Between 1997 and 2004, 11.3% of all 3- to 17-year-olds living in poverty were identified as having a learning disability, as opposed to 7.9% of children from households above the poverty line (Child Trends Data Bank 2007). Is it possible that teachers are reaching out to learning disability specialists to intervene with those children whose only disability is low school readiness?

Before the NCLB Act of 2001, in many schools, children with learning disabilities were educated in self-contained classrooms at a pace commensurate with their ability to proceed. Since the enactment of NCLB, teachers have been expected to bring even the most disabled children up to grade level to meet year-end testing accountability. LD children are mainstreamed along with their normally developing peers, and educators struggle between choosing a pace that allows the disabled to keep up with the curriculum framework, leave them behind, or stop and reteach, performing a disservice to those students who are ready to move forward. These hard choices distress dedicated educators who fear their level of commitment and effectiveness will be judged solely by their students' test scores.

When we look at the numbers of low SES students identified as LD, we must also look at the possibility that the learning problems of a substantial number of children with LD placement can be accounted for, at least in part, by the lack of school readiness—not a true discrepancy between ability and performance. According to a report published by the National Education Summit (1999), more than half of failing schools, as determined by state competency exams, were in urban areas. Of these, 40% had minority enrollments that exceeded 90%, and 75% were high-poverty schools in which

- the majority of students qualified for free lunches;
- teachers tended to be younger and less-qualified, and teacher turnover was high;
- resources, such as well-stocked libraries and up-to-date technology, were lacking;
- connections with parents were often nonexistent or hostile; and
- absenteeism and delinquency were high.

In urban schools that enroll high percentages of low SES students, two-thirds or more of students fail to reach even the basic level on national tests (National Education Summit, 1999). As teachers struggle to overcome these seemingly impossible roadblocks and face higher and higher standards to achieve Annual Yearly Progress (AYP) under NCLB, they may find themselves making more and more referrals of students for learning disability placement.

Many educators feel that NCLB has taken the focus away from meaningful education and placed it solely on meeting AYP to avoid being labeled a failing school and the possibility of losing federal education funds. Many schools seem to be concentrating on following the litany of rules attached to NCLB rather than seeking ways to provide deep, meaningful, innovative instruction. If a school fails the AYP guidelines for two years, parents are given the right to choose an alternative school. This not only abandons the struggling school, but forces parents to make a choice between their neighborhood schools and those outside familiar surroundings to which their children may be bussed. Parents who are already struggling with time and transportation issues in their neighborhood schools face even higher barriers in trying to become active shareholders in a school that is some distance away.

Parents who choose to leave their children in their neighborhood schools and opt for the tutoring programs mandated for failing schools under NCLB soon find the inherent disadvantages to this facet of the law. Viadero (2007) reports that George Farkas, the Penn State University scholar who wrote the chapter on tutoring for NCLB, stated that the tutoring being offered is too little, too late. According to Farkas, it's reaching only a fifth of the eligible students and producing little or no gains in achievement. The programs are poorly funded and mismanaged. Students in tutoring programs generally receive instruction after school, when participation isn't always possible, in small groups of about five to seven, and they generally drop out of the program at about 40 hours of instruction. He recommended that in order to optimize the possibility of closing the educational gap, below-grade-level students should be served with at least 100 *individual* lessons for 40 minutes per lesson to gain a grade-level size boost.

Many Title I schools provide excellent education but struggle to overcome the myriad issues associated with the effects of the poverty that allowed them to originally be identified as Title I schools. The focus on the noble, but extremely unrealistic, aspirations of NCLB—that every child will be proficient in reading and math by 2014—has detracted from the type of school improvement that could eventually turn education around (Hess & Kendrick, 2007). There hasn't been funding for foundation building in the form of full-day kindergartens, preschools in high-poverty areas, parent education, intervention rather than remediation, or meaningful staff development to educate teachers about the social and educational implications of poverty or programs that foster higher-level thinking skills in children. Our bias is that these types of initiatives would provide students and their communities with lifelong skills instead of spending time teaching to a test that will make no significant difference once the test is over.

Proponents of NCLB argue that the federal government has provided preschool opportunities for families in low SES neighborhoods. Yes, there is Head Start, but once again, this is a program put in place without the muscle required to make it work. In 2001, only 12% of children nationwide were enrolled in Head Start (Currie & Neidell, 2003). This represented only slightly more than half of the children who were eligible. Furthermore, the similarity to the lack of funding behind NCLB is alarming. While Head Start makes an effort to introduce social skills, healthy habits, and parental involvement, teachers' low pay and low levels of education seriously constrain program quality (Ripple, Gilliam, Chanana, & Zigler, 1999; Zigler & Styfco, 1994). Schools can't meet 100% of the requirements in reading and math when only 50% of the preschoolers are receiving the foundational support they need to succeed in the future.

We recognize that not all low SES students start out behind their more affluent peers. Some children certainly overcome societal barriers and come to school with intact readiness skills. However, there's evidence that even when they start out ready to learn, their low SES status may threaten their success in succeeding years. Gerwertz (2007) tells us that the "Achievement Trap" study, conducted by Civic Enterprises LLC and the Jack Kent Cooke Foundation, urged education policy makers to take a long, hard look at high-achieving, low-income children and pay attention to the fact that, without intervention, over time, their achievement often takes a downward trajectory that can cancel out the strong start they demonstrated earlier. The children from low-income homes who score in the top quartile in nationally normed tests upon school entry come to school with on-target, but weaker, academic skills and environments not always conducive to supporting their strengths. By fifth grade, 44% of these originally high-scoring first graders tend to drop out of the first quartile. This is 13 percentage points higher than those students whose family income is over the national median of $48,000.

With NCLB, the federal government mandated perfection in American schools by 2014. While this is a lofty goal, it may be a nearsighted theory built on a foundation of quicksand. On an international scale, America has the highest percentage of children living in poverty of the 24 countries that comprise the Organization for Economic Cooperation and Development, and we've held that dubious distinction for the last 10 years (Viadero, 2007). When we consider the failure of our society to provide decent health care, adequate housing, and public safety for a majority of the disadvantaged students who attend our most challenged schools, is it surprising that many children are struggling, and schools have a difficult time complying with NCLB? We believe that the focus on accountability through NCLB has caused panic and distress and eliminated the reflective aspect that any movement toward reform requires. It seems to us that without a thoughtful look at the causes of our educational failures, well-constructed, developmentally sound approaches to reform and courageous, innovative ways of addressing the specific needs of low SES children our schools—and even NCLB or any other scream for educational excellence—will be silenced without success. We think there are better ways to address the problems of low school readiness suffered by low SES children in our public schools.

SUMMARY

A number of important factors challenge us to provide equal education opportunities for all of our students, including those from low SES homes. These include diversity, poverty, lack of parent involvement, educators' deficit perceptions, and the accountability demands of NCLB. As difficult as these challenges are, especially for schools in low SES neighborhoods, we believe there are effective means to overcome them and ensure all of our students are well served in regular classrooms in their neighborhood schools.

2

The Unfortunate Link Between Low Socioeconomic Status and Learning Disabilities

Our goal in writing this book is to encourage and enable those of you who work with children of low socioeconomic status (SES) to provide every child in your school with equal opportunities to achieve their maximum academic potential. The statistic that really caught our attention was the fact that a much higher percentage of low SES children are referred for placement as learning disabled than their middle- and upper-class peers. We're all for addressing the educational needs of children with diagnosable disabilities, but we worry that low SES children are shunted off on the special education track when it's not only unnecessary but also frequently harmful. In an effort to "get you on the same page with us," this chapter takes a hard look at what we see as an unfortunate, but identifiable, link between low SES and learning disabled (LD) placement.

As you read this chapter, please note, as we have, that there's a time gap between some of the research regarding links between low SES and learning disabilities and the study we'll discuss in the upcoming chapters. That gap clearly suggests to us that perhaps low SES children have, both in fact and in viable research, been "left behind."

Also, please note that none of our discussions in this and other chapters should be interpreted as suggesting that we believe all children who live in low SES neighborhoods are equally affected by all of the problems and educational barriers presented by low SES. We are *not* promoting any stereotypes: We are presenting statistics that clearly identify that many problems exist for way too many of these children that we, as educators, need to address.

UNDERSTANDING LEARNING DISABILITIES

To understand the link between learning disabilities and poverty, we need to look at our history of addressing disabilities in our schools and the frustrations that have arisen as we have struggled to enable every child to succeed in school. Despite compulsory education laws that had been in place nationwide since 1918, until the third quarter of the 20th century, many children with disabilities were routinely excluded from public schools. In general, their options were to remain at home or be institutionalized. And those with mild or moderate disabilities who did enroll in public schools were likely to drop out well before graduating from high school (Pardini, 2002).

The 1954 *Brown v. Board of Education* decision, which extended equal protection/rights under the law to minorities, and the civil rights movement of the 1960s paved the way for similar gains for children with disabilities. In the 1960s, parents of disabled children, who had begun forming special education advocacy groups as early as 1933, undertook concerted political action to improve educational opportunities for their children. Finally, in 1975, Congress passed the Education for All Handicapped Children Act, better known at the time as Public Law 94-142, to guarantee disabled children's right to a full public education.

Public Law 94-142 proved to be landmark legislation. It required us to open our public schools to students who exhibited a broad range of disabilities—physical handicaps, mental retardation, speech, vision and language problems, emotional and behavioral problems, and other learning disorders—and provide them with a "free appropriate public education." Moreover, the law called for school districts to provide this schooling in the "least restrictive environment" possible. Reauthorized in 1990 and 1997 and renamed the Individuals with Disabilities Education Act (IDEA), over the years, the law has resulted in the delivery of services to millions of students previously denied access to public education. Because of IDEA, students with disabilities could not only attend school but also, at least in the best case scenarios, were assigned to small classes where specially trained teachers adapted instruction to meet each student's individual needs. The law also required schools to provide any additional services as needed, such as interpreters for the deaf or computer-assisted technology for the physically impaired, to help students reach their full potential. And, in more and more cases, special education students began spending time every day in regular classroom settings with their non-special-education peers in the least restricted environment. All of us were expected to learn how to meet the special needs of these children in our classrooms—unfortunately, in most cases, without adequate additional training.

Learning disability definitions have evolved over time. History suggests the term *learning disabilities* originated with and became popularized by the writings of Dr. Samuel Kirk in the early 1960s. Kirk used the term at the 1963 "Conference on Exploration into Problems of the Perceptually Handicapped Child," and in 1968, in the First Annual Report of the National Advisory Committee on Handicapped Children, headed by him, he wrote,

> Children with specific learning disabilities exhibit a disorder in one or more of the basic psychological processes involved in understanding or in using spoken or written languages. These may be manifested in disorders of listening, thinking, talking, reading, writing, spelling, or arithmetic. They include conditions, which have been referred to as perceptual handicaps, brain injury, minimal brain dysfunction, dyslexia, developmental aphasia, etc. They do not include learning problems which are due primarily to visual, hearing, or motor handicaps, to mental retardation, emotional disturbance, or to environmental disadvantage. (Kirk, 1963, p. 2)

The learning disabilities label was formally adopted by Congress in Public Law (PL) 91-230, the Elementary and Secondary Amendments Act of 1969. PL 94-142 formalized the definition, and the current IDEA definition remains unchanged from PL 94-142. Consequently, the definitions of learning disabilities have *excluded* environmental factors that may contribute to low achievement and poor performance.

Originally, the concept of specific learning disabilities referred to a particular subgroup of students who didn't achieve academically commensurate with their ability, presumably because of a central nervous system dysfunction that was prominently reflected in a wide range of psychological process disorders. The use of the word *specific* in the definition implied that a discrete and circumscribed condition was present instead of a generalized failure that would be more closely associated with mental retardation (Kavale, 1995). However, soon after this definition was recognized, it became apparent that two features, *central nervous dysfunction* and *process disorders,* were difficult to establish with consistent reliability. In their place, academic failure is now defined by *discrepancy.* Discrepancy is the primary criterion we use for LD identification. While the definition may not be consistently understood or applied, LD is typically defined on the basis of a severe discrepancy between ability and achievement not caused by some other specified condition. An LD child performs poorly because of difficulty in one or more of the following areas: listening, speaking, reading, written expression, mathematics, and reasoning. The discrepancy for this child is described as *unexpected,* while the discrepancy in a child with mental retardation is *expected* (Gresham, 1996).

Studies (Foehlinger, personal communication, January 12, 2006; Fuchs & Fuchs, 1995; Ysseldyke, Algozzine, Shinn, & McGue, 1982) show that learning disability results from a compromised central nervous system function that inhibits or disrupts the learning process. The main indication of learning disability is a discrepancy between a child's measure of potential ability, or IQ, and the child's measured manifest ability, or academic achievement. Low achievement indicates a performance that is one standard deviation below the norm for a given population, regardless of ability. On the other hand, *underachievement* refers to performance that demonstrates a marked discrepancy between a child's ability and performance. This is important because, using this definition, we can distinguish learning disability from low achievement that may originate in social and economic disadvantage.

Learning problems that result from social and economic disadvantage are referred to as *low achievement* and are believed to represent a discrepancy between age and achievement only (Ysseldyke, Algozzine, Shinn, & McGue, 1982). For example, a child who is a low achiever in a third-grade classroom is performing below other third graders in a specific content area or areas. Low achievement, then, represents low academic functioning independent of ability and doesn't imply a specific causation (Gresham, 1996). For children exhibiting low achievement, achievement is discrepant with age but not with IQ, as both IQ and achievement are below that expected for the child's age. Furthermore, unlike LD, which is defined as originating from cognitive dysfunction, low achievement is a condition that can result from adverse environmental factors associated with poverty.

Underachievement, however, is believed to be caused by low aptitude. For example, if a child has a low aptitude in reading, that child may have an IQ ability of 100 but is performing in reading at 75% of grade level. This may be an indication of a learning disability in language or another area that affects reading (Foehlinger, personal communication, January 12, 2006). While specialists in the field of learning disabilities may not agree consistently on the definitions for low and underachievement, as educators we know the frustration of trying to provide the right services for children without fully understanding the cause of their learning problems.

Presently, the LD category is the largest segment of special education and receives the most appropriated funding. The number of children identified as LD has steadily increased since the recognition of LD as a disability. Many think that the continuous increase in the number of students identified as LD may well indicate ongoing uncertainty regarding the difference between underachieving students with and without the LD label (Algozzine, Ysseldyke, & McGue, 1995; Fletcher, Shaywitz, Shankweiler, Katz, Liberman, & Stuebing, 1994; Kavale, 1995; Kavale, Fuchs, & Scruggs, 1994; Pennington, Gilger, Olson, & DeFries, 1992; Ysseldyke, Algozzine, Shinn, & McGue, 1982). The bottom line is that there has been a steady increase in the number of identified LD children. Specifically, over the last 20 years, the rate of special education placement for children with learning disabilities has more than doubled. In comparison, the overall increase in the public school student population has risen by only 12.6% (Hoffman, 2002; Lewit & Baker, 1996). This naturally raises the following questions in our minds:

- Why have we seen a higher number of students identified for learning disabilities than the increase in the student population generally?
- Could it be that we have highly accurate testing protocols to diagnose the areas of speech/language deficiency, mental retardation, and emotional disturbance and do not have a definitive measurement for learning disabilities?
- Are we using the LD category to obtain extra assistance for our struggling low SES students?
- Is LD identification a reflection of the lack of school readiness some children bring to school and the school's inability to address the issue, or is it truly a learning disabilities issue?

POVERTY IS NOT A LEARNING DISABILITY

It's disheartening to look at the statistics of child poverty in the United States. This country has a significantly higher incidence of child poverty than any other western nation, and the numbers have continued to rise over the past 20 years. For the past two decades, child poverty levels have varied between 10% and 20% of the population, with the prevalent trend toward the higher numbers. There was a slight decline during the late 1990s, but a steady increase resumed starting in 2000. Large numbers of children currently live below or near the poverty line. In fact, 37% of all American children live in poverty-level households, including 42% of infants and toddlers, 58% of Black children, and 62% of Hispanic children (National Center for Children in Poverty, 2004).

Numerous studies have demonstrated that the consequences of being poor can be significant and have lifelong effects. Low SES children are much more likely to have life experiences that are educationally damaging as compared to their higher SES counterparts. Poor children are much more likely to have low birth weight, prenatal drug exposure, poor nutrition, lead exposure, and personal injuries and accidents.

In addition, there appears to be a relationship between poverty and LD identification. It seems to us that if low SES/poverty were *unrelated* to LD placement, the identification rates among low SES children would mirror the rate of growth of the general population; however, this isn't the case. A study conducted in Florida (Blair & Scott, 2002) examined the relationship between economic disadvantage and LD placement for children born between 1979 and 1980. Analyses of the survey data indicated that 30% of LD placements of boys and 39% of LD placements of girls were attributable to what were identified as low SES markers, such as exposure to violence and drug use, poor-quality child care and schools, absence of routine dental and medical attention, and lack of adult-run recreational facilities The data showed that the risk of LD identification was significantly higher for children affected by *any one* of these low SES markers than for those children who weren't.

A Department of Education Report to Congress (U.S. Department of Education, 1997) also noted that increased childhood poverty has implications for special education. "As poverty has increased in the United States, the number of children with disabilities who receive special education has also increased" (p. 20). The statistics in most of the studies underlying the report indicate that the steadiest growth in special education was in the learning disabilities category.

Does special education simply mirror what society expects of children of poverty? Are low SES children fated for special education and learning disabilities? There's a greater likelihood that children of poverty who are labeled "at-risk" will experience arduous childhoods. At-risk children are assigned to government-supervised programs, such as Head Start, and early childhood special education (Polakow, 1993). This leads the referral process to ignore the broad context in which children live and the factors that determine ability and disability. Sigmon (1990) proposed that decisions about students who are poor "merely replicate class biases that are skewed against students who are poor" (p. 14). While poverty is only one risk factor, it intensifies all other risk factors.

The risk factors of low SES children and connections between disabilities and low SES continue to be evident. Studies (Blair & Scott, 2002; Harry, 1994) have shown that a substantially higher percentage of children who were diagnosed with learning disabilities lived in families in which incomes fell below $25,000 and that the LD placements of a substantial number of children may have an origin that is, at least in part, generated by the lack of school readiness and schools' attempts to remedy this lack of readiness by labeling students as LD in order to receive outside support.

EDUCATORS' LACK OF UNDERSTANDING OF POVERTY

When children's experiences don't match teachers' and principals' expectations, many attribute school problems to "deficient" environments and lower their expectations for the students' success. Unfortunately, they sometimes fail to recognize economic differences that affect children's learning styles. For example, children from lower socioeconomic backgrounds may not embody independence and intrinsic motivation. Some of these children fail to perceive their own efforts as an important cause of success or failure. These students will not be successful unless we teach them using strategies compatible with their cognitive orientations.

When we place children in situations that don't fit their prior experiences, for which their background has not prepared them, or just simply don't interest them, they may develop a "reactive stupidity" that's quite different from the way they think and act in their own homes and neighborhoods. Such children are then at risk to fall behind, become truant, and drop out because the school experience appears useless or irrelevant to them. If we don't understand why these children behave as they do, we may incorrectly attribute their lack of academic success to a learning disability instead of to their reactive approach to avoiding failures they feel unequipped to control. For example, our expectations that children who are often surrounded by chaos at home can sit still and focus in a school setting is, perhaps, unrealistic. Studies from as far back as 1991 that have examined programs for at-risk preschoolers conclude that preschoolers from low-income families need help preparing to participate in large academic groups, complete seatwork tasks independently, and make effective transitions between classroom activities (Carta, 1991).

TEACHERS' ROLE IN LEARNING DISABILITY REFERRALS

The numbers suggest to us that educators too often view special education placement as an easy way to provide special instruction to low-achieving children whose families can't afford outside tutoring. Unfortunately, once the

LD label is applied, few children exit this educational track. The difficulty in distinguishing between students with true learning disabilities and low-achieving students may be an inability to recognize social behaviors as precipitating elements in the referral process. This is unfortunate if at-risk factors are viewed as disabilities, and the effects these factors have on children's academic success or failure are ignored. Once children are identified as having a "disability," the responsibility falls to special education teachers to help the children achieve. If economic and foundational issues go unnoticed and unaddressed, special education is not really a viable remedy.

Research data suggests, in part, the choice of teacher may significantly affect the probability that students will be referred for special education services. According to research conducted in nine elementary schools in grades K–3 (Gottlieb & Weinberg, 1999), one-eighth of the teachers made two-thirds of all referrals. The researchers also found that students' behavior, not significant delays in their academic achievement, was a factor in their referrals. President Bush's Commission on Excellence in Special Education reported that 10% of teachers referred more than 80% of children placed in a high-incidence category, such as LD (U.S. Department of Education, 2003). Another study (Drame, 2002) identified several teacher variables that have a potentially significant influence on classroom teachers' referral tendencies and their perceptions of problematic student behaviors. For example, perceptions of a learning disability as being an academic disability are related to a tendency to view aggressive behaviors and temperament-related behaviors as disruptive to classroom management. These perceptions lead many teachers to refer students for LD identification more often when confronted with negative temperament-related behaviors.

As principals and teachers, we have specific expectations for what students should be ready to do and what behaviors they should exhibit. Our expectations of the skills and abilities that students bring to school should be grounded in an understanding of child development and how children learn. If we base readiness expectations on a rigid array of skills and competencies, however, and focus only on a few facets of development, the multidimensional aspects of growth can be missed, and children who are well within the normal range of development may be labeled as behind or disabled (National Association for the Education of Young Children, 1995).

While we routinely devise strategies to meet the needs of well-behaved, low-achieving students, we may be less willing when children have behavioral issues. In a school that has a consistent number of low SES students in each classroom, why do some teachers have higher referral rates than others? Children from low socioeconomic backgrounds may exhibit behaviors that have no correlation with academic ability, but are linked instead to family instability, poverty, transience, and weak academic preparation. Research suggests that a number of these sociocultural factors may impact teachers' referral decisions. For example, Kauffman, Wong, Lloyd, Hung, and Pullen (1991) explored teachers' reasoning related to classroom behavior and labeling children at risk for school failure. Their study examined how sociocultural factors impacted teachers' judgments regarding children's academic success. The results indicated that teachers highly value those behaviors that relate to good academic performance—that is, positive work habits, compliance, and motivation—and, in general, have negative reactions to highly aggressive and noncompliant behaviors that interfere with classroom routines.

In fact, social and behavioral deficits, instead of classroom performance, may be the major factor influencing low SES students' initial referrals for LD placement. Today, children entering kindergarten face higher goals, more demands, and more formal instruction than ever before. Those of us who work with young children know that some children are more ready to meet these demands, based on the wide variety of experiences they encountered prior to school, while other children may react negatively to the same demands and respond in ways that are unacceptable in the classroom. For example, educators who work with children from low SES backgrounds often note that these children are more likely to externalize behaviors than are children from higher socioeconomic backgrounds (Dodge, Petitt, & Bates, 1994). When behavior is out of sync with their expectations, teachers may tend to look for a learning disability as the cause. A number of researchers have reported that almost half of all referrals of children as LD in urban schools involve misbehaviors and not academics (Gottlieb, 1985; Gottlieb & Alter, 1994). Could this be why we refer more boys? Boys are more likely than girls to be identified as having a learning disability (Child Trends Data Bank, 2007).

A number of researchers have addressed the suggestion that teachers' referrals for LD testing are influenced more by low tolerance for negative behaviors than by students' lack of academic ability. Drame (2002) interviewed high-referring teachers and found that while a single behavioral incident wouldn't always prompt a referral, any single incident could be seen as "the last straw." Gresham (1996) noted that it's difficult to distinguish between low achievement and learning disability because some misbehavior may be directly related to learning problems, for example, in the case of attention deficit hyperactivity disorder (ADHD), or simply brought about by the inability to keep up and the frustration and anger that can result from failure. In addition, factors such as ethnicity may strongly shape teachers' closeness to students. Alexander and Entwisle (1988) found that social distance between teacher and student may also influence educators' expectations of academic performance, eventually impacting student performance.

Poor academic progress and misbehavior appear to be frequent causes for student referral, but a third cause is also likely. During teacher interviews, conducted as part of their study of referring teachers of low-functioning students, Gottlieb and Weinberg (1999) found that teachers reported they sometimes believed students had given up trying to learn and referred students for LD testing because they appeared to be disconnected from the learning process and were no longer interested in education. Can an apparent disconnection from education legitimately be called a learning disability? In several studies, different teachers reacted differently to low-performing students, resulting in substantial discrepancies in the referral rates of teachers (Gottlieb, 1985; Gottlieb & Alter, 1994). In any case, teachers' tolerance of misbehaviors, student engagement, and low performance seem to be strong components in the final decision regarding who is and who isn't given the LD label.

Yet another factor is deficit perception that's produced solely by teachers and becomes a self-fulfilling prophecy. Alexander, Entwisle, and Thompson (1987) found that the teachers they studied who came from higher socioeconomic backgrounds tended to have lower expectations for minority and poor children, and these teachers frequently rated minority and poor children lower on behavior assessments and maturity. Unfortunately, many students who underperform on traditional assessment tools become victims of their teachers' deficit perceptions concerning their learning abilities. Teachers who assume that low SES students come to school with learning problems frequently offer these students watered-down curricula, boring lessons, mindless tasks for homework, and rote memory skills instruction. Based on their deficit perception, these teachers immediately think in terms of remediation rather than education for their low SES students. Teachers' prior judgments can be extremely damaging to children in the first years of school, when school motivation is being developed. Furthermore, early school success or failure often forecasts future school achievement. By the time we start looking at possible reasons for school failure and lack of academic progress in our students, generally second or third grade, low SES Black students are 3.0 times more likely and Hispanic students are 1.2 times more likely to be referred and identified for special education (Child Trends Data Bank, 2007).

A referral by a teacher doesn't automatically place a child in an LD program. Schools are required by federal and state laws to have multidisciplinary evaluation systems, which include parental permission for each student. However, the chances that a child who is referred for evaluation will eventually be identified as LD is significant. In one study, 88% of the students referred by teachers were found to be learning disabled and eligible for services (Gottlieb, Gottlieb, & Trongone, 1991).

THE COST OF MISIDENTIFYING CHILDREN AS LEARNING DISABLED

Available data about school enrollments and program funding nationwide is invariably out of date by the time it's published. So, to talk about the financial cost of the misidentification of low SES students as LD, we'll have to work with what's available and extrapolate a little. In 2003, the U.S. Department of Education estimated that in 2002, nearly 6 million students between the ages of 16 and 21 received special education services under Part B of IDEA. Most, 67%, of those students were diagnosed with either learning disabilities or speech/language impairments (*Education Week,* 2004). During the same period, federal funds supported 7.5% of the total special education expenditures at the local level (Chambers, Parrish, & Harr, 2002). The rest of the support came from the states and local school districts.

The Child Trends Data Bank (2007) reported that, in 2004, the average per-student cost was $7,552, and the average cost per special education student was an additional $9,369, or $16,921. That means that in 2004 it cost more than twice as much to educate a special education student as it did a regular student. Under IDEA, the federal government is committed to paying 40% of the average cost for educating special education students. However, in this decade, the actual federal funding has been closer to just 20%. That means that local taxpayers have been responsible for the lion's share of the cost of providing special education services. We feel safe in suggesting that the cost of educating both regular and special education students has not gone down in the past four years but rather has risen and will continue to rise.

Greene and Winters (2007) noted that, from 1977 through 2002, spending on special education services almost doubled due to the fact that the number of special education students increased by 76%. With LD placements increasing from 796,000 in 1977 to nearly 3 million in 2003, LD represented a particularly costly segment of the special education budget. A recent report published by U.S. Department of Education (2008) shows that from 2001 through 2005 nearly half of all special education placements were in specific learning disabilities. In 2005, 2,780,218, or 45% of all special education students (ages 6–21), received LD services. The cost that year to educate 5.2% of the total student population consumed 11% of the total education budget (U.S. Department of Education, 2008).

We're concerned that, if teachers are misidentifying low-achieving low SES students as LD, they're effectively funneling scarce education dollars away from both regular education programs and those that serve the truly disabled. Given the fact that many school districts nationwide are facing budget cuts due to the current slump in our national and state economies, wasting (and we use such a strong word purposely) available education dollars on misidentified LD students makes no sense. What makes more sense to us is to focus available education dollars on improving the education opportunities of low SES students in regular classroom settings.

The cost of misidentifying low-achieving low SES students as LD is not just manifested in dollars. Another statistic that got our attention is that, in spite of the continuously increasing number of LD placements, many children continue to fail. In 1995, the reported dropout rate for LD students was 17.6%. In 2003, only 34% of exiting learning disabilities students received a diploma (U.S. Department of Education, 2008). To us, there doesn't appear to be a positive correlation between identifying children for LD services and the likelihood that they'll be successful in school, even with the extra services and the label. A growing number of educators posit that when children's at-risk factors are labeled as deficits, the role these factors play is ignored. Since we can identify at-risk markers, wouldn't it be more beneficial to children who are struggling in school to identify the markers and put interventions in place to address these factors before moving to special education identification?

Children who are identified as LD have special education teachers assigned as their case managers, and their Individual Education Plans (IEP) form the basis of their education. The list of adaptations and accommodations that can be provided for LD children is endless. While these accommodations are legitimate for the truly learning disabled, when applied to low-achieving students, they frequently serve to water down curriculum, lower expectations for students, rob children of intrinsic motivation, and foster a deficit perception that is damaging for a lifetime.

The deficit perception is not only held by the teacher but can be internalized by the child and adopted as a norm by the child's parents. Most children, unless impeded by cognitive impairment, are born ready to learn. They're curious and eager to explore their environments. When they enter school, most children are excited to learn. When children entering school are asked if they're smart, they'll boastfully explain how smart they are and will often overestimate their cognitive abilities (Nicholls, 1979; Stipek, 1992, 1999). As first graders begin to get feedback from their teachers, they become much more aware of how they compare to their classmates. If they start to struggle, they may begin to see themselves as less competent than their classmates. Subsequently, they may begin to question their academic ability, enjoy school less, and lose motivation over time (Stipek, 1992).

Once a label has been assigned, many children begin to mirror the attributes they associate with that label. How many of us have heard a child say, "You know I can't do that, I'm LD," or "I have to go to summer school because I'm stupid." When we water down the curriculum and children are not challenged, when they honestly feel they can't compete with their peers, and when their "shortened" assignment is finished before others in the class finish their "regular" assignments, they frequently turn to behaviors that are annoying or distracting to other children and foster a negative impression that supports the deficit perception. The loss of education dollars due to mislabeling a child as LD is painful, but the loss of a child's ability to believe in him- or herself is beyond computation.

When teachers misidentify low-achieving low SES students as LD when the children's real problem is the lack of background knowledge and school-readiness skills, we miss the opportunity to formulate a strong diagnostic approach to identifying the real problems and putting meaningful, effective teaching strategies and techniques in place. When children's struggles in a classroom are attributed to a learning disability, the social environment in which the students operate for most of their lives is unexplored. One of the first things most of us learned in our education psychology courses is Maslow's (1943) hierarchy of needs, which illustrates that people's motivation to achieve is directly related to their needs—those that are being met and those that aren't. The needs Maslow identifies, in ascending order of importance, are physiological safety, security, love, esteem, and self-actualization. People's needs at each level must be met before they're motivated to seek further goals. When children's difficulties are viewed as caused by a learning disability, these needs may go unaddressed, and the motivation to learn and succeed may be cut short. When we look at the numbers of low SES children who are misidentified as LD rather than enabled to overcome their low school readiness and succeed in the regular classroom, the cost in lost opportunities is great indeed.

SUMMARY

To clarify our concern about the number of low-achieving low SES children who, we believe, are misidentified as LD, we first reviewed the definition of specific learning disabilities incorporated in IDEA, the federal legislation that addresses special education. According to that definition, *learning disability* is underachievement caused by a specific central nervous system dysfunction, and *underachievement* is defined as a significant discrepancy between ability and achievement—between IQ and test results for example—based on a physical dysfunction. *Low achievement,* on the other hand, describes a discrepancy between age and achievement that is unexpected (and unrelated to a physical dysfunction), which may well result from social and environmental disadvantage. Then, to understand why a much higher percentage of low SES children are identified for LD placement than their higher SES peers, we looked at the attitudes and tendencies of teachers—who predominately represent middle-class backgrounds—that researchers have found to be related to their special education, and particularly LD, referral decisions.

Finally, we described the significant financial and educational costs of the misidentification of low-achieving low SES children as LD; the former as a burden borne by the federal, state, and local governments, and all of us as taxpayers; the latter in terms of the education opportunities lost to low SES children. When inappropriate and unnecessary LD remedies are applied and the root causes of these children's learning problems go unaddressed, nobody wins. Since we can identify the at-risk markers that can cause low achievement among low SES children, it's to everyone's advantage for us to do so and then to address them. The remaining chapters in this book present our findings about how this can be achieved.

3

Teaching Strategies and Techniques Proven to Work With Low SES Children

Our first two chapters focused on the evidence that (1) children from low socioeconomic status (SES) environments are identified as learning disabled (LD) at a rate that far surpasses the rate for children in general and (2) shunting low SES children off onto the special education track results not only in a financial drain on our public school systems but too often damages these children's egos, stifles their creativity, stunts their intellectual growth, lowers their teachers' expectations for their learning ability, and reduces their future chances to reach their full potential. We posited that many low SES children are low achievers in their early school years, not because of a diagnosed learning disability, but because they start school lacking many of the readiness skills they need to thrive in the classroom. We noted that there's solid research that suggests that, because of their lack of school-readiness skills, many low SES children exhibit behaviors in the classroom that are at best unproductive and at worst seriously disruptive. And it's often because of their behaviors that teachers refer them for identification as LD.

When you look at our public schools nationwide, it's clear that the majority of teachers come from middle-class environments and economic backgrounds. We believe that this fact may adversely influence teachers' expectations of low SES students. Table 3.1 lists only a few of the possible *disconnects* between teachers' expectations for low SES children and what those children bring to their classrooms. As minimalist as the table may be, it should ring true with those of you who work with low SES children.

We think understanding the home environment of low SES children is critical to working with them, especially when you realize how much time children generally spend in their home environments as opposed to the school environment. Look at the math. In general, the school year is 180 days (minimum) and the average school day is, say, 6.5 hours long. That's 1,170 hours a year. A normal year contains 365 24-hour days. That's 8,760 hours. Children's time in school represents only 13.4% of their time. To us, this means that we must include the home environment in all of our thinking, planning, and interacting with all children and especially low SES children.

Some teachers, recognizing the sources of problematic classroom behaviors, refer low SES students for LD placement as a means to get tutorial help, which their parents are unable to provide, for these students. This is understandable but not the best answer. Others simply see them as children who can't succeed in the regular classroom, assume that they are LD, and refer them for special education identification. Again, understandable, but not the answer. We contend, and there are many education researchers who agree with us, that low SES children are not less intelligent or less able to learn; many just simply start school without the requisite skills they need to behave and learn effectively in a classroom setting.

So how do we enable low SES children to succeed in school and avoid misidentification as LD and the serious human and financial costs associated with that misidentification? School districts across the country are trying a wide range of approaches. Some major cities have turned their entire school systems over to private companies that promise rapid turnaround in student achievement. Other districts have turned schools in their lowest-income neighborhoods either into charter schools run by private organizations that can employ resources and teaching methodologies not available in the standard curriculum or into magnet schools designed to capitalize on children's specific talents or interests to engage them more successfully in their own education. Other school districts are experimenting with merit or incentive pay plans on the theory that, if they can pay the most effective teachers more money, they'll be able to keep the best teachers teaching and motivate the less-effective teachers to either "do better" or leave the field of education. Still other districts are looking at ways to eliminate the tenure and seniority provisions common to teaching contracts to enable staffing decisions to be based solely on putting the

Table 3.1   Possible Disconnects Between Teachers' Expectations and the Reality of Low SES Students' Home Environments

Teachers' Expectations of Students' Backgrounds	Reality of the Environment of Many Low SES Homes	Common Problem Behaviors of Many Low SES Children
• Daily activities are well planned and scheduled and include many routines. • Children are encouraged and enabled to enjoy a wide variety of experiences under the supervision of their parents. • Children learn to trust that their needs will be addressed, even if they have to "wait their turn."	• Parents' work situations are less stable and may include multiple jobs and difficult scheduling conflicts. • Life is lived "moment to moment" rather than according to a reliable schedule or routine. • Children can't count on "their turn" coming in any predictable time frame.	• Lack of trust in adults. • Inability to sit still for extended periods of time. • Reluctance to "try new things." • Reluctance to share time, space, or resources with other children.
• Parents provide wide range of educational resources, including learning/study time, work space, basic equipment and materials, books, and supervision. • Children are fed regular meals and get a full night's sleep.	• Learning resources may be severely lacking. • Parents may not be home to provide either encouragement or support. • Regular meals and time and space to get a good night's sleep may not be available.	• Inattention in class (due to hunger and/or fatigue?). • Failure to complete homework assignments. • Lack of preparation for classroom activities. • Refusal to participate in some activities.
• Parents talk to their children; family communication is primarily verbal. • Children are encouraged to express themselves and to expand their vocabulary and their understanding of words. • A key message is that if you work hard at whatever you're doing, you'll succeed, and achievement of goals is rewarded.	• "Family time" may be very limited, and the opportunity to learn verbal communication skills may be slim to none. • The first language of the parents may not be English. • Children may learn to react primarily to nonverbal cues to guide their actions. • A key message may be, "Do what you need to do to get by."	• Lack of verbal skills. • Unwillingness to "keep trying until you get it right." • Nonverbal responses to questions and instruction.
• Children are taught from their earliest years to follow the instructions of parents and other adults. • Parents provide frequent positive feedback as a means of encouragement. • Children are encouraged to ask questions about things they don't understand, and parents are more than willing to provide answers.	• Because of parental work schedules and other demands on their time, parents are less likely to provide instructions and supervise children's ability to follow them. • Parental feedback is less frequent and more likely to be negative than positive. • Asking questions of parents is more frequently discouraged than encouraged.	• Defiance or unwillingness to follow instructions. • Distrust of positive reinforcement. • Failure to ask questions when needed to complete work assignments.

right teachers and administrators in the right places. In addition, universities, other research institutions, and private companies have produced hundreds of staff-development and classroom-improvement systems school districts can purchase and implement to improve instruction and student achievement.

We don't question the quality of the research or the sincerity of the intentions of these various efforts. But with our combined 75 years or more of experience in the field of public education, we suggest that there's a simpler, better, and more cost-effective solution to improving the education opportunities of low SES children. In this chapter, we discuss classroom strategies and techniques that we've seen to be notably effective in integrating low SES children who entered school lacking critical school-readiness skills into the standard education program, without resorting to special education (LD) intervention. Our recommendations are based on a study conducted in 2006 (Howard, 2007) in one of the largest school districts in Virginia. This district is located in the greater Washington, D.C., metropolitan area and serves students from some of the highest-income neighborhoods to some of the lowest-income neighborhoods in the state.

The focus of the study was to discover what elementary school teachers of low SES children, who have the lowest rate of referral for LD placement, do that's so successful. The study sites were a number of elementary schools in which at least 40% of the students were eligible for free lunch programs (low SES by definition). The student populations of these schools were also primarily minority, including Blacks, Hispanics, and a wide range of Asian and Middle Eastern cultures. The teachers who participated in the study were recommended by their principals based on the fact that, over the previous three school years, they had

- referred no more than one student per year for LD identification;
- retained no more than one student per year; and
- ended each of the school years with all their students at or near grade level in achievement.

The participating teachers completed an initial questionnaire, participated in both individual and group interviews, and were observed and videotaped in their classrooms over a period of three months. As we analyzed the data from the study, we were able to categorize their effective teaching methods into four common strategies that were implemented in all of their classrooms:

1. Building positive relationships with students and their families

2. Conducting formative and summative assessments of their skills

3. Integrating learning experiences

4. Creating a positive climate for instruction

Now, we'll be the first to admit that there's nothing new or revolutionary in these strategies. They're part of fundamental, accepted education theory and practiced by truly effective teachers everywhere. What struck us when we looked at the study data was the consistency with which all the participating teachers employed all of these strategies all of the time, and the fact that the children in all of the classrooms we studied were achieving at or near grade level by the end of the school year, regardless of the level of school readiness skills they possessed on the first day of school. We contend that if all elementary school teachers *understood* and *consistently practiced* these four strategies in their classrooms, the level of student achievement in even our most troubled schools would be greatly enhanced, and many fewer low SES children would be misidentified as LD. As we look more closely at these strategies, we anticipate you'll come to agree with us that staff development programs focused on enabling all of our teachers to understand and implement these strategies in their classrooms may well be a far better use of school district dollars than purchasing expensive programs.

FOUR TEACHING STRATEGIES THAT WORK

Building Positive Relationships With Students and Their Families

Like the exemplary teachers we observed, we put relationship building as the first and most important strategy for working successfully with all children, and especially low SES children. We believe that the quality of the teacher-student and teacher-parent relationships is the key to student achievement. Because we discuss the school-home relationship in the next chapter, in this one we focus on the relationships developed by teachers with their students.

Perhaps most critically in the primary grades, children's relationships with their teachers can significantly affect their self-confidence, their eagerness to learn, and their whole attitude about school and its relevance to their lives. If we want our students to achieve in the classroom, building strong working relationships with our students needs to be our first priority.

Think back for a moment about your favorite elementary school teacher. What was it about him or her that you loved and remember to this day? While each of us may use different words to describe what we felt about that favorite teacher, we suspect that some common denominators would be comments like, he or she

- knew who I was;
- cared about me and my classmates as individuals;
- gave me all kinds of encouragement when I had trouble with something;
- never made me feel "stupid";

- made me feel important;
- made everything understandable and fun;
- was always fair and treated everybody the same.

When teachers develop and maintain positive relationships with their students, the students trust, respect, and look up to their teachers and work hard to earn their trust, respect, and approval in return. Like all interpersonal relationships, positive teacher-student relationships don't just happen. They take real effort to develop and constant attention to maintain over time.

We all remember our first days as student teachers and how intensely we worked to make a positive impression on our students and earn their respect, their attention, and their willingness to learn what we wanted to teach them. We worked hard to learn not only their names and faces but also who they were as people. We needed to understand their strengths and weaknesses and their personality quirks so that we could figure out how best to teach them. After all, our careers were absolutely on the line! If our lesson plans failed and the children didn't learn the lessons successfully, then we would fail.

Exemplary teachers, like those who participated in our study, approach every school year and class with this "student teacher mentality." They see their own success inextricably tied to the academic achievement of every one of their students. They make the effort every day to learn as much as they can about their students and use that knowledge to build and maintain a positive working relationship with each of them. The only thing they take for granted, the only preconceived notion they bring to the classroom, is that, as Corbett (2002) put it, "While I agree that prior knowledge and motivation vary from child to child, I believe that all can learn given the proper environment and teaching strategies in my classroom. It's a challenge, but we can make a difference" (p. 14).

The teachers we observed in the study fully accepted their mandate to ensure that their students were constantly learning, without exception, without excuses. They all agreed that the onus for students' achievement rested on their shoulders. It was up to them to figure out how to teach so the children could learn the lessons. They all stressed the "getting-to-know-their-students aspect" of their philosophy. One commented, "We have to connect with these kids. We can teach all we want, but you have to know what's going on with them, in and out of school, before you are going to reach them." Another firmly believed, "It's not their fault if they aren't getting it. I have just got to think of a better way to do it in that case." "You need to reach out," said another. "If the parents don't know how to help the kids, then, teach them too." The teachers were not only focused on getting to know the students but getting to know them as a whole—their parents, their hobbies, their experiences, their hopes, and their fears. One expressed it nicely when she said, "Just get to know each child well enough so you can find something to celebrate. Whether it's sitting nicely, trying hard, singing a song, or good handwriting, find a reason to celebrate that child in front of the whole class."

These teachers set high goals for all of their students, and once those were reached, they set higher ones. They were never quite satisfied that this was the best a child could do. They approached low SES children's economic barriers not as something that was wrong with the children, but as indicators of the support the children might need to succeed.

Today, just as when we were student teachers, we understand that building positive relationships with all of our students is the key to enabling them to achieve academically. In our minds, the other three strategies discussed below are foundationally integral to this all-important relationship building.

Conducting Formative and Summative Assessments

The exemplary teachers we studied unanimously believed that accurate assessments of students' skills and abilities were critical to the teachers' understanding of how to support and guide their instruction. They noted that the integration of performance and feedback has proven very helpful to students as they work to develop their understanding of a particular topic or concept. In the teaching for understanding framework, it's called "ongoing assessment." To us, ongoing assessment is the process of providing students with clear feedback regarding their growing understanding in a way that will help them to improve their next performance. In their classrooms, these teachers continuously assessed the learning progress of each student and employed strategies swiftly to address areas of weakness. They noted that using ongoing assessment can improve teaching and learning by providing timely feedback, and that frequent assessment of student achievement enables them to adjust instruction, effort, and practice, and enhance students' potential to succeed. Whether it was a change in their teaching strategies or calling in resource specialists, they didn't allow time to elapse or content to pass without knowing if learning had occurred. They worked to ensure that there would be no surprises at the end of the year.

These teachers all appreciated the districtwide program that provides for a preassessment of kindergarteners to gain insight into their needs and identify foundational gaps. They felt that knowing what the children would initially bring to school helped them gain a deeper understanding of the home support, education level of parents, and the level of intervention they might need to provide. They also believed in the use of portfolios that follow students through the grades and give successive teachers previews of their incoming students. They noted that having portfolios over the summer months would be beneficial and leave more time for review and planning.

Many education researchers agree that portfolios are particularly useful for ongoing assessment, noting that they provide concrete evidence to document growth over time. In this way, they help students, teachers, and parents appreciate individual students' accomplishments, regardless of how they compare to other children or to grade-level expectations.

The instructional methodology of the exemplary teachers we observed is data driven, and they used the data to shape their instructional planning. They stressed the importance of using every form of assessment available to them to accurately gauge their students' progress or the lack thereof, and they noted that they used a variety of ongoing formal assessments. Among these were the Developmental Reading Assessment (DRA), Phonological Awareness and Literacy Screening (PALS), Star Reader Assessment, San Diego Reading Assessment, Early Childhood Assessment Program (ECAP), and various math inventories. They all said that they relied on accurate documentation of assessment results to provide resource teachers with clear rationale when they needed to request intervention. In addition to formal assessment tools, they also used informal assessments to monitor growth and identify learning gaps. These included such techniques as running records, memos, and games they created to put the children at ease and allow for a stress-free observation of skills.

The fluidity of information from grade to grade will vary in all of our schools, but each of us can seek out the academic background information on incoming students and prepare assessment information to pass on to the next teacher. We all know that discipline records are readily available! A child's history of preferred learning style, areas of strength and weakness, and effective strategies that were used in the past should always be available so each year teachers can "hit the ground running" with each child without spending six weeks or so getting to know their students.

As educators, we need to view assessment as a valuable tool to measure the degree to which learning is taking place in our classrooms. It's not enough to say, "85% of my class passed this test." Can we afford to ignore the 15% who didn't? Using formative assessments routinely provides us with a gauge for individual children, as well as the group. Formative assessments should not be used for grading but for guiding ongoing instruction. Placed logistically along the path of instruction, such assessments can help us accomplish several strong education goals. If we review students' work products and test results routinely, we can learn whether we need to change the tempo of instruction, retreat and reteach, or move ahead. There may be times when we can skip content because formative assessments tell us that the children already have the content in place, and we can move on. This leaves time in the instructional schedule to go back and reteach a different skill or content that wasn't mastered. In cases where the majority of students fail to grasp a concept, it's definitely time for us to retool the teaching strategy and collaborate with colleagues about possible new approaches. Once the new measures are set in place, we need to continue using formative assessments to identify students who may still not be grasping the content.

When our assessments indicate there's still a persistent, small number of students who are unable to internalize the information, we must use available resources to provide the necessary support for them. In this situation, we don't recommend, for example, that an instructional assistant pull the students out during math class to revisit past instruction they didn't master. This practice only serves to ensure that these children will be behind again in the new instruction. All instruction at this point needs to be in addition to, not in lieu of, the regular classroom lessons.

To gauge whether students are instructionally sound enough to progress to a new chapter in social studies, a foundationally higher concept in math, or an extended piece of writing, we need a summative assessment that wraps it all up. Like formative assessments, summative assessments should not be administered solely to provide a report card grade. If we have used formative assessments to guide us through a content block and have retaught, restructured, and provided support for those students who were struggling, and the summative assessments tell us we still have students falling behind, we need to examine the foundational information that was lacking in order to teach the new content, the academic point at which we began instruction, and even the possibility of a learning disability that requires more concentrated intervention.

So often teachers lament, "I don't know why those children did so poorly. I taught it." We must remind ourselves we're *not* in school for *teaching;* we're there for *learning*. Student learning is the only result that counts! Consistent use and analysis of assessments of learning will clearly help us know when our students are learning and when *they're not*.

Integrating Learning Experiences

The literature supports one compelling fact: What students already know about the content is one of the strongest indicators of how well they'll learn new information relative to the content (Marzano, 2004). The "knowing" can take various forms. By being cognizant of the background knowledge your students bring to the classroom, you can integrate material from their already developed schematic formations into the new information being presented. This building on the already known can give us an already well-paved path to new learning instead of trying to build new roads on undeveloped territory.

The teachers we observed used three specific techniques for integrating their students' learning experiences: linking what is known to what is unknown, promoting discovery learning, and integrating instruction.

Linking What Is Known to What Is Unknown

There are two terms that are often used interchangeably, *background knowledge* and *prior knowledge*. For the purpose of assessing the foundation of our students, we should consider the differences between these two terms. Prior knowledge takes into consideration the totality of students' learning and experiences. It's not content-area specific and is overarching. Prior knowledge is related to the environment, home language, cultural customs, religious beliefs, and family dynamics, to name just a few contributing factors. Background knowledge has a more finite meaning and is directly associated with the background knowledge a child has in relation to a specific topic. This may be a child's experience with the zoo, traveling on a train, reading maps, and so on. One of the teachers we observed told us that it's important that we accurately assess both of these areas of understanding in our students because there's a definite demarcation in the educational process of children when they stop learning to read and begin reading to learn. The amount of prior and background knowledge students have can be directly linked to the success they'll have in committing new learning to long-term memory where it can be stored and manipulated for continued use across the curriculum.

Elementary school students are confronted daily with new content and struggle to associate it to something in their schematic framework in order to organize and comprehend incoming information. To transition effectively from the learning-to-read stage to the reading-to-learn stage, children need strategies for associating new material with learning already in place. By associating new knowledge with existing understanding, students gain the ability to construct new meanings, change previous perceptions, and develop new frameworks to support higher levels of thinking and use of knowledge. When students lack adequate background knowledge, or are not provided with the stimulus needed to enable them to access this knowledge, they begin to encounter difficulties participating in and progressing through the general curriculum.

Education researchers have suggested that by assessing students' previous knowledge with a background questionnaire, a pretest, or other method (Angelo & Cross, 1993), you're taking a learner-centered approach to your teaching (National Research Council, 1999). If you know what they know, you're much better able to connect the course content to their previous knowledge. The process begins with some key questions because the contemporary view of learning is that learners construct new knowledge and understanding based on what they already know and believe (Cobb, 1994). The teachers we observed acknowledged that the responsibility for assessing the degree of background knowledge that's present is theirs. They said that they begin by asking themselves these questions:

- What background information do my students need to be prepared for what I am teaching?
- How can I best assess their background knowledge?
- What resources are available in my school to help students who need background enhancement?

Once we accurately assess the amount of knowledge in place, as constructivists we can activate and build upon background knowledge. The teachers we observed used several effective techniques for assessing and activating background knowledge:

- Using a recall approach and asking students to tell, write, or draw what they know about a given topic. Asking students, "What do you already know about farms?" gives you an opportunity to assess their understanding and to activate ideas they may not have thought about.
- Establishing "talking buddies" or small "experience groups" in the classroom in which students can share their knowledge with each other and then with the entire class. This not only affords students the opportunity to share their experiences; it gives every student access to additional knowledge in a learning-community format.
- Previewing questions to determine and activate background knowledge. By asking students to put themselves in the shoes of a main character in a story and predict intentions, outcomes, or purposes, you can assess their familiarity with a topic or story outline.
- Using the K-W-L approach (what I Know, what I Want to Know, and what I Learned) to stimulate a meaningful dialogue with the students prior to instruction and create a summary vehicle following instruction. In this way, students can speak to their immediate understandings of the topic and voice their curiosities about what they want to learn. Learning becomes a journey of discovery and sharing that has purpose.
- Using videos, film clips, field trips, and content-related pictures to increase background knowledge through vicarious experiences. For example, spend 10 minutes at the beginning of an agricultural unit viewing various farming methods in different locales with an explanation of how this links to upcoming instruction to help inner-city students gain some insight to an area with which they have had no experience at all. Follow up with a short period of verbal sharing to ensure students can articulate what was new to them or ask questions about things they may have viewed but not understood.

One area of concern when assessing background knowledge is being aware of the accuracy of the knowledge students have internalized. Faulty background knowledge can be as useless as no background knowledge at all. If a child knows that the West is part of the United States but believes that cowboys and Indians still roam the land, their background knowledge is faulty and will need to be updated.

The teachers we observed agreed that accurately assessing the amount of background knowledge present and becoming adept at altering their content starting points is one of their most important roles in supporting their students' success in the classroom.

Promoting Discovery Learning

Eureka, I've found it! Discovery learning is based on this "aha!" phenomenon. Discovery learning takes place when students are placed in a problem-solving mode and challenged to find their way out. It allows children to draw on their own experiences and prior knowledge to discover the answers to new problems. It's an internal process that becomes a personal triumph and creates a constructivist classroom environment.

All of us have experienced the joy of an "aha" moment when we successfully overcame a mental hurdle or solved a puzzle. For many children from low SES homes, battles are not easily won, and victories may be few and far between. Allowing students to use their personal prior and background knowledge in classroom learning activities validates their experiences and tells them that their background and culture have value and purpose. When a child can explain the color of a flower by associating it with the color of a fire hydrant on his street or convey the sound metal makes by the clank of a token deposited on a metro bus, he learns that his life experiences have the same value as anyone else's.

Discovery learning affords children the opportunity to use their own experiences to reach conclusions that make learning more vivid and better internalized. New learning is inevitably built on previous knowledge, and the teachers we observed continually probed for connections between the knowledge each child had and the content at hand. For example, if a child had never been on a boat, they looked for alternatives as basic as asking them if they'd ever played with a toy boat in the bathtub or seen soap float in a sink.

Another technique they used to encourage students to use what they already know in a new learning situation was to ask probing questions such as the following:

- What do you think will happen next?
- What does the cover of this book make you think of?
- Why do you think he did that?
- How did you reach that decision?

These questions probe for understanding while pushing the cognitive process for exploration. Not only do they stretch students' thinking processes but also build a positive sense of self.

Discovery learning may take either of two forms depending on the age and cognitive ability of the students. In some cases, we can use a form of experimentation that gives our students a certain degree of freedom to solve a problem. This type of discovery learning needs to be accompanied by well-planned clues and a stable framework that will prevent students from going too far a field and becoming mired down in confusion and tangential thinking. For younger learners, a more expository form of discovery learning provides students with a well-prescribed path to follow to a conclusion already predetermined by us.

Discovery learning affords students a certain degree of control over their learning experience, encourages them to employ higher-level problem-solving and thinking skills, and promotes the building of deeper and richer schematic foundations for use later, when background knowledge is once again needed to support new learning. We believe that Socratic learning theory and discovery learning theory have common roots, that is, thinking is not driven by answers but by questions.

Integrating Instruction

Integrated instruction is the practice of seeing education as weaving the fabric we call learning. Every thread relies on the strength of those surrounding it. Every content area is supported by, and contributes to, the understanding of the entire educational experience. Integrated instruction is a valuable technique to develop patterns of understanding for students. And this can have broader benefits for low SES students as they begin to discover relevance and interconnectedness not only between school experiences but between school and home experiences as well.

There are several ways to integrate instruction in our classrooms. One that was very important to the teachers we observed was the development of students' study skills across all areas of the curriculum. Recognizing that most children don't know how to learn, they taught those skills and guided the students' use of them regardless of the content of the lesson. Among the skills they teach are

- listening to directions,
- asking questions for clarification,
- observing,
- identifying similarities and differences,
- drawing conclusions,

- using mnemonic devices,
- identifying available outside resources,
- verbalizing what they've learned,
- taking notes for future reference, and
- memorizing.

While the standard curriculum lesson plans to teach these skills may be limited to specific content areas (observation in science, mnemonics in social studies, memorization in language arts or math, for example), the teachers we observed consciously and routinely reminded their students of these skills and encouraged them to apply them in all subject areas. We heard statements or questions like the following:

- Do you remember when we studied the leaves in science and tried to see what was the same among them and what was different? Can you use the same skill to see what's the same and what's different in the clothes the pioneers in this picture are wearing compared to the clothes we're wearing today?
- This morning in math we practiced adding. Can you "add up" the clues in this story and tell us the answer to the little boy's question?
- Let's read the instructions at the top of the worksheet together before we begin. Does everybody understand the directions? Any questions about what you're going to be doing?

These teachers believed, as we do, that teaching children how to learn is their most important responsibility. Consciously teaching these skills is one way to improve the educational opportunities for low SES children.

Another form of integration that's equally important in the classroom is content integration. Math is relevant to science, science complements social studies, and language arts skills are imbedded in all areas. While the teachers we observed allotted specific time each day to the various content areas, they routinely linked lessons learned in one area to other areas to both reinforce the earlier learning and use the background knowledge to enhance understanding of the new lesson. In one classroom in a social studies lesson on the western expansion of the United States, children were asked to use multiplication, measuring, and other related math skills to compute the speed, direction, and miles traveled by wagon trains. In other classrooms, teachers set up guided reading groups during science, social studies, and other language-heavy content areas to provide students with leveled readings on the topics. While teaching nutrition during a health class, another teacher asked the students to build a diet within a certain calorie limit, estimate how many calories were burned with routine exercises, and determine whether the diet provided the recommended daily requirements of certain nutrients. The teacher gave the students visual strategies to use such as Venn diagrams, charts, and tables. This lesson integrated math, science, and physical education into one lesson. In a fifth-grade classroom, we observed collaboration with a PE teacher on a lesson plan related to the establishment of the 13 colonies. The names of the states were taped, in ascending order, to the climbing wall, and children were asked to climb in the order that the colonies were developed. There were very few fifth graders who couldn't tell you the order of settlement by the time everyone finished! Integrating content from the various subject areas not only reinforces learning of the content material but also demonstrates the relevance of different content areas to students' daily lives.

"Themeing" is another technique for integrating learning experiences and helping students appreciate the interrelatedness of what they're learning. In one of the schools we observed, the fourth-grade teachers focused all of the lessons for a week on water. The teachers collaborated and agreed to teach some chapters out of sequence in order to present this theme fluidly (pun intended) across the content areas. The students studied water and soluble materials in science, the American rivers in geography, the early settlements along our Atlantic coast in social studies, and measuring water and water displacement in math. The students were excited about the week and full of ideas about other ways to include water in their studies.

Creating a Positive Climate for Instruction

The learning environment is the "weather" that affects virtually everything that transpires in the classroom (Tomlinson, 2004). A positive learning environment doesn't just happen: We create it. Our goal should be to ensure that every child who enters our classrooms feels safe, validated, individually important, and successful. To accomplish this, the classroom design, teacher's feedback, schedules, classroom rules, discipline practices, and resources must all be geared toward promoting academic success.

The teachers we observed used a number of classroom management techniques that produce a positive climate for learning, such as what follows.

Creating a User-Friendly Classroom

Sometimes our students, particularly those from low SES neighborhoods, live in homes that are disordered and confusing. They may have moved several times. Perhaps there's no private place for them to keep their school supplies and personal things or no quiet place in which to study. Several of the teachers we observed set aside a small area of the classroom with a couple of bean bag chairs to provide restless children with a calm place to go and read for a short period of time when the pressure of the classroom became too much to bear. They regulated the use of the chairs and ensured that children didn't use the quiet corner as an escape from classroom responsibility. This took some time and attention on their part, but they reported that the decrease in acting-out behaviors more than made up for the extra effort.

These teachers emphasized the importance of keeping their classrooms well ordered with all supplies and instructional materials easily accessible to students to maximize instruction and minimize time spent retrieving supplies. They made sure that pathways around the room were clear so children could move about to various locations with ease. They also consistently laid out work on individual desks before their students arrived in the morning to provide them with a purposeful learning activity as soon as their day began. We observed that posters, bulletin boards, and graphic organizers were all clean, intact, and visible, sending the message to every student that the room is ready for education.

The teachers we observed consciously used the seating arrangements in the classroom to complement the format of their teaching and foster student learning. A number of these teachers changed seat assignments periodically to mix things up a bit and provide the students with a new view—a different perspective—on the classroom. They aligned seats differently to best suit the instructional format and the needs of their students. They liked the desks in a semicircle, whenever possible, so that all students would feel they were contributing members of the class, and there would be no one to hide behind. When small groups were expected to work together, they moved the desks to face each other in small pods to stimulate face-to-face discussions. They arranged the desks in single or double rows for demonstrations or projects and when students needed to be engaged in totally independent work.

The teachers we observed used the physical aspects of the classroom to enhance learning and took advantage of the walls and bulletin boards to display learning aids. Depending on the age of the students, these included the alphabet, multiplication tables, parts of speech, sentence structures, and other simple basic facts to give students reference points when needed. These were of particular help to children who hadn't had repetitive exposure to these foundational facts and hadn't had the opportunity to commit them to long-term memory. By keeping these facts constantly visible, they promoted students' internalization of them.

A key element in a user-friendly classroom is the security students feel when they know what is expected of them and what the consequences will be if they fail to meet those expectations. While commercially produced posters of classroom rules may look bright and colorful, the teachers we observed believe that children feel more secure when they have been part of the process of developing classroom expectations. Low SES students, in particular, may live in neighborhoods where they don't feel physically or emotionally safe. The teachers we observed involved the students in the *process* of developing the classroom behavior rules—gave them a voice regarding what makes them feel unsafe and hurt and an opportunity to verbalize the rules that would make them comfortable. The rules, in fact, didn't change much from year to year, but every class could take personal ownership of them.

In addition to the framework of known expectations, another element of a user-friendly classroom is consistency in classroom routines and academic and behavioral expectations. Consistency, without rigidity, provides a structure in which students can feel safe and secure. This is true for all children, and especially for low SES children, whose home environments may be somewhat unpredictable or unstable. Child psychologists agree that children need to know what the "boundaries" are. The more consistently the boundaries are reinforced, the easier it is for children to work within them. They can focus on the lessons without wondering or worrying about what's coming next.

Consistency with regard to expectations for academic achievement and student behavior also translates, in children's minds, to fairness and confirms their sense of equality with their classmates. Children develop a sense of fairness long before they enter kindergarten and react negatively both when they perceive they're being treated unfairly and when they see others being treated that way. The teachers in our study routinely communicated their expectations and classroom routines and used the same words or phrases to refer to them every day. Even when working individually with students, they kept an eye on what the rest of the students were doing and never failed to correct inappropriate behavior or acknowledge good behavior.

Creating a Democratic Learning Environment

A democratic learning environment is one in which students are engaged and active participants in the learning process. In such an environment, students are seen as peer educators who share knowledge rather than as mere containers waiting to be filled with information. It's a learner-centered approach in which students choose some of their daily activities, or the way some activities are pursued, that helps create a sense of community within the classroom. The teachers we observed provided many opportunities for their students to create songs, stories, poems, timelines, games, and interactive notebook interpretations of what they are learning from the lesson. They also provided opportunities for shared decision making with their students on a level commensurate with their students' age. They all agreed that providing students with choices that are manageable tends to motivate the students to work toward completion. Among the kinds of decisions they let their students make are letting them choose whether they work at their desks or sit on the floor, vote for the read-aloud book of the week, take notes with green ink or blue, do the math problems on page six or seven for homework, and demonstrate their knowledge either by writing a poem, creating a picture, doing a project, or putting on a skit with likeminded classmates. Even the lowest-performing children will participate when the choice is theirs, and they take pride in the final product.

A number of the teachers we observed said that the approach helped to create a supportive environment that allows different cultures to permeate the instruction and lead the class in ways they hadn't foreseen. They also noted that the resulting sense of community and equality appeared to break down the hierarchy of socioeconomics in their classrooms, giving everyone a voice.

One of the teachers pointed out that providing students with a means to express their feelings about their learning can provide us with valuable information about our teaching and their progress. For example, at the end of a lesson, this teacher gave each student a small index card like the one below.

Our Study of Dinosaurs
Name:
In the lesson about dinosaurs, I liked when we
And I didn't understand the part when we
Next time we talk about dinosaurs, I would like to

This provided his students time to think about what they'd learned and start using some metacognition about what they think would make their learning more productive.

Another important choice that a number of the teachers gave their students was the degree to which they participated in certain activities. While they always asked their students to share their work, they never forced them to do so. If a child declines, they said, we let them know that, when they're ready, we look forward to hearing about what they learned. When there is no sense of urgency or press for performance, they find that children soon learn that mistakes are okay; there's no need to choose the "easy" book or simplest project as a way to avoid errors, and their work products are as good as their classmates'.

Providing Positive Feedback Early and Often

Positive feedback is a powerful tool in the classroom not only because it helps children build self-confidence but also because it tells children when they're going about the task the right way, giving them permission to keep going. The teachers we observed all used positive reinforcement in the form of kind, reaffirming words, smiles, appropriate touches and hugs, and praise to provide the children regular and timely feedback on their efforts, both when they achieved success and when they made progress toward it.

Using positive feedback appropriately isn't as easy as it might seem. The most effective praise is communicated to the student directly, refers specifically to the praiseworthy behavior demonstrated or result achieved, and is delivered as close in time to the event as possible. When you affirm and validate the children's positive behaviors and achievements, avoid using the word *but*. Statements such as, "You used pretty colors but they are outside the lines," negates your first words of praise. Children generally internalize the last statement they process.

The same thing is true when the feedback is corrective. We don't mean negative feedback here. Children need to know as soon as possible if they're not meeting your expectations, before their misbehavior or academic error becomes a big problem. Corrective feedback should always be communicated discretely and directly to the child and refer to the specific behavior and not the child.

As they try to find their places in the world, children absorb words, feelings, actions, and beliefs and internalize them. When children hear words of praise and encouragement, they learn to love and respect themselves. When they receive constructive corrective feedback, they learn that it's okay to make a mistake as long as you correct it.

Every child benefits from frequent appropriate feedback, but it may have special significance for children from low SES environments. The average child from a professional family receives 32 affirmative replies for every 5 disapprovals, a ratio of six to one. In sharp contrast, children from low SES homes hear 5 affirmations for every 11 disapprovals, a ratio of one to two. Simply put, children from more affluent homes are rewarded for speaking, and children from low SES homes are not. The latter are clearly expected to take commands and be silent (Hirsh-Pasek, Golinkoff, & Eyer, 2003). We must make sure that doesn't happen in our classrooms.

Providing Verbal and Nonverbal Cues

Verbal and nonverbal cueing is an effective technique to gain the attention of the students and stay in fluid communication with them throughout the day. Using cues helps students to understand the message you're trying to send and keep them on task. You can, for example, use verbal cues to

- prepare students for impending transitions: "You have three minutes to finish your pictures before we go to PE";
- remind them of procedures: "I will call on anyone who raises his or her hand";
- deter misbehaviors: "What are the classroom rules?" "How should we be acting while we are on the story carpet?" "Are you all keeping your hands to yourselves?"
- sustain attention: "One, two, three—eyes on me," or "Listen up, I am going to give directions";
- allow a child to prepare for answering: "I am going to call on you after Mary," "Tommy, I'll come back to you in two turns so you have more time to think of a great answer."

Verbal cueing before changes in the action in the room works to focus children on what's happening at the moment and mentally prepare themselves for what's coming next.

The teachers we observed routinely used verbal cues to signal that they were about to communicate something very important: "Class, I have something very interesting I want to share with you," or "Michael, I am going to tell you something very exciting." They used similar cues to redirect misbehavior, and when doing so, they immediately told the students exactly what they expected of them so that their expectations were clear and not left up to speculation.

The teachers also used nonverbal cues to great effect. When confronted with a student who frequently had a difficult time paying attention in class, one of the teachers met with the student before class and worked out a nonverbal cue that only the two of them would know and use between themselves. When the teacher noticed that the student was off task, she used the signal by pointing two fingers to her eyes and then to his eyes. When he saw this signal, it was a cue to get working. No one else was disrupted, and he went back on task. Another teacher, who had a student who constantly talked to his neighbor, used a nonverbal cue of walking over to the student's desk and placing his hand, palm down, on the desk. He extinguished the behavior without losing his teaching momentum and without causing the child any embarrassment.

Using your physical presence to establish proximity to students can be a valuable technique in creating and maintaining a classroom in which students feel comfortable and stay on task. The days of lessons being delivered from a raised desk at the front of the classroom are long gone. Your closeness to your students can serve as a nonverbal signal of protection, strength, and identification. Standing near a student who's having some difficulty can communicate that he or she is not alone in the struggle, and positive affirmations such as "You are on the right track; I know you can get this" provide meaningful support.

The teachers we observed rarely sat at their desks. They constantly moved around the room. When they needed to remind students to settle down and get back to work, they stood near them, or they walked up and down a row of desks as a subtle way to intercede before a student acted up too much. When they wanted to praise or correct a student, they bent down to the child's level to communicate support. And they made sure that they spent some time near every student every day. The message was clear: "I'm here with you to help you achieve everything you can." Not everything needs to be said with words. As we all know, sometimes the things we don't say communicate clearer than words could have.

Structuring Time Effectively

Understanding both the amount of time that children can sit still and focus and the need for interaction on a regular basis can go a long way to prevent classroom frustration and misbehaviors. Many children from low SES homes haven't experienced sustained periods of time when they are expected to sit still to listen to a book being read to them, learn their alphabet, or practice writing their names. At home, they may govern their own time to a large extent and may easily abandon a task at school when it becomes difficult, switching their attention to something less frustrating. When we require that children sit still for 30 minutes while we lecture to them, we're asking for the restive responses we often encounter. Kindergarteners' productive attention span is about 7 to 10 minutes. For elementary school children, it's approximately 10 to 15 minutes, and for teens, about 20 minutes. Pushing these limits is too often counterproductive.

The effective teachers we observed maximized their classroom time fully by making sure that the room was organized, lesson plans were well prepared, and work tables, easels, and so on were prepared and in place. They planned their lessons so that periods of instruction were interspersed with periods of movement and "fun" activities. And they recognized when a lesson had tested the patience of the class and adjusted their timing. They worked with their students' attention spans rather than against them. By avoiding boredom and restlessness that can result in misbehavior, they maintained a busy, productive, interesting learning environment.

These teachers also recognized the importance of making a smooth transition from one learning activity to the next. Although children certainly recognize the sound of the bell as a signal to quit a learning situation and move on to recess, lunch, or home, if they are engaged in one learning activity and need to move to the next, the transition may not be so clear. Parents who have called their children in from playing outdoors or from the TV set to dinner know this all too well. Shifting mental gears is a learned skill, not an innate one. While children who've grown up with multiple well-scheduled routines at home may have learned to switch gears more quickly, children from low SES homes may have far less sense of schedules and timing. They may need a clearer signal to tell them what's coming next and what's expected of them in the meantime.

These teachers also often used a timer for the last five minutes of an activity and let the children know that when the timer buzzed it would be time to change activities. They made sure their students knew what would be coming next. They recognized that a simple statement such as "The timer for math has been set. You have five minutes to finish your work, put your book away, and get ready for recess" can give an apprehensive or insecure child needed guidance and time to adjust his or her thinking.

Cultural and Academic Flexibility

One of the most important facets of a positive climate for learning is flexibility, both cultural and academic. By this we mean adapting quickly and actively to new and changing situations to capitalize on students' strengths to promote, and mitigate any hindrances to, students' educational development. Earlier in this chapter, we pointed out some of the many disconnects that can exist between teachers' expectations regarding the home life of their students and the realities of the environments in the homes of many low SES students. Most teachers, we believe, have never experienced their low SES students' realities. They haven't lived in a house with no heat in the winter or run out of food stamps before the end of the month. They haven't experienced actual or imminent homelessness. In general, their parents were available to pick them up after school activities and to help them with their homework. They didn't have to rely on their parents' ability to fill out and return free lunch applications to be assured of a good breakfast and lunch, just to name a few.

As principals, we need to make sure that our teachers are not only aware of the significant difficulties their low SES students may face outside of school but also encourage and enable them to respond to and mitigate these difficulties. In the schools we observed, the teachers were empowered to address individual students' needs in ways not anticipated by the prescribed curriculum or standard classroom practices. The teachers we observed frequently sidestepped standard practices to address the realities of their students' lives in an effort to ensure that the home lives of their students didn't limit their educational opportunities. Here are a few examples of actions we observed these teachers take to level the playing field for their low SES students.

- They arranged for a parent of another student to give a child a ride home so the child could participate in an afterschool play rehearsal.
- They called the PTA to request money for a student's lunch until the free lunch program application was filed and processed.
- They set aside time at the end of the school day for homework to provide assistance to students whose parents couldn't.
- They established a dialogue with parents so that the parents would feel comfortable to talk with them about changing situations at home that might affect their children's ability to participate.
- They borrowed a coat from the school counselor so a child could go out to recess with the rest of the class.
- They allowed a student to take a 15-minute nap in the nurse's clinic after learning that the child hadn't been picked up from the sitter's until after 10 p.m. the night before.
- They allowed a fidgety child to sit on the floor instead of at her desk.
- They conducted the regular parent-teacher conference by telephone when neither parent could get away from work.
- They called the employer of three students' parents and offered to advertise his business in the next school newsletter if he'd give the three parents paid time off to attend teacher conferences.

When teachers are *encouraged* and *enabled* to respond to problems their students may experience outside of school, the students' energies can be focused on learning. And for low SES students, the difference can be significant.

Flexibility is also a productive technique to enhance academic success. As we observed these successful teachers of low SES students, we became increasingly aware of the similarity in their approaches to academic flexibility. They all assessed their students' prior and background knowledge and adjusted their teaching based on the amount of background knowledge they'd need to introduce before instruction began. They also adjusted their ability groupings and the amount of time allocated for instruction of each concept. And they routinely retaught lessons that weren't learned by all students the first time around—even when it meant postponing the next unit for a time.

The teachers we observed also practiced differentiation of instruction. *Differentiation of instruction* is the means by which teachers effectively respond to the variations in learning styles and abilities of their students. By differentiating instruction, teachers vary their teaching to create the best learning experience possible for all students. You can differentiate at least four classroom factors based on student readiness, interest, or learning profile:

1. *Content*—what you require the student to learn or how this learning will be accessed.

2. *Process*—the method, practices, or activities the student will engage in while attempting to master the content.

3. *Products*—the proof that will be presented to verify that learning has occurred.

4. *Learning environment*—the way the classroom works and feels.

Differentiation is *not* dummying down the curriculum for weaker students or having lower expectations of low SES students, minority students, or children with disabilities. The teachers we observed

- learned as much about each student's knowledge and skill base, abilities and interests, preferred learning style, and so on, and conducted regular formative and summative assessments to understand the children's strengths and weaknesses as fully as possible;
- started each student's learning from where he or she was in terms of knowledge or skill level and tailored the content of lessons to capitalize on each child's knowledge base to maximize the opportunity for the children to learn the concept, process, or technique being taught;
- incorporated a variety of learning activities designed to appeal to the full range of learning styles of the students;
- wherever possible, tailored the work products required to capitalize on each student's interests and talents;
- consciously developed a learning environment in which differences were not only accepted but were acknowledged and appreciated; and
- provided opportunities for students to share their learning experiences with other students to help students internalize their own learning and benefit from what others had learned.

Employing a Sense of Humor

Humor is a basic and important human emotion, and there are significant links between positive emotions and learning. As Mary Poppins famously sang, "a spoonful of sugar makes the medicine go down," and humor is certainly a form of "sugar" we all use to lessen tension, build community, and enable learning. Just look at the remarkable amount of learning television shows like *Sesame Street* and *Dora the Explorer* have produced for generations of American children.

As we said earlier, the era of the stern schoolmaster or schoolmistress who ruled the classroom with a willow switch or wooden ruler is long gone. A little comedy can bring a lot of joy and learning opportunities to the classroom. You don't have to act like one of the Three Stooges, but some humorous antics can go a long way in creating a happy environment. For some children, it may be a duplicate of home, but for others, it may be a new experience. It's difficult for children to be fearful or insecure when they're happy, smiling, and laughing.

The teachers we observed all incorporated humor in their classrooms. While some were more boisterous and energetic in their use of humor than others, they all used themselves as foils for jokes, mistakes, and corrections. Some made silly faces and let out boisterous cheers, while others were subtler in their humor. Many shared anecdotes from their own childhood. One broke into a silly song once in awhile to signal the end of a test. Bringing a smile to any child is an opportunity to make a classroom fun and safe and reinforce the message that learning is, in fact, fun.

Celebrating Students' Successes

One of the most powerful motivators for all of us is recognition for a job well done. One of the key concepts in Blanchard and Johnson's (1982) classic management book, *The One Minute Manager*, was the power of praise delivered personally by managers whenever they "caught" an employee doing something right. Recognition not only feels good at the moment but also serves to build our self-confidence and motivate us to top our own performance in the future. Children are no different, in this respect, from adults.

Celebrating the successes of both individuals and groups in the classroom produces multiple benefits. The obvious ones are the good feelings and ego boosts the successful students experience at the moment of celebration. The broader benefits are that classroom celebrations

- communicate to the students that they are each important and that someone cares, notices, and appreciates what they achieve;
- demonstrate that working hard to achieve goals has meaningful rewards;
- create a sense of community and show the benefits of working with others; and
- graphically illustrate that learning is fun.

The teachers we observed celebrated classroom victories often. From a simple "high five" or "fist bump" with a child who finally solved a difficult math problem, to a class party or outing to recognize the successful end of a unit or good test results, these teachers took every opportunity possible to celebrate learning and recognize the successful efforts of their students.

SUMMARY

We don't believe that poverty is a learning disability or that children from low SES environments can't enjoy the same level of educational success as their peers from more comfortable economic situations. We looked at the practices of a number of teachers who have proven over time that the low SES students in their classrooms can succeed when they use the strategies and techniques we've discussed in this chapter.

We believe that the educational opportunities of low SES children can be enhanced in any school that's willing and committed to changing the primary focus of ongoing staff development from "student achievement" to "teacher achievement." When teachers use a one-size-fits-all lesson plan, you always run the risk of leaving low SES children behind. The teaching strategies and techniques we've discussed here will work well with every child, but they are especially effective in overcoming the school-readiness needs of low SES children. And the good news is that these strategies and techniques can be implemented on a classroom-by-classroom basis and are cost-free ways to make a difference in the educational success of the all the children in your school.

4 The Importance of Strong School-Home Relationships in Educating Low SES Children

Experts agree, and we do, too, that effective education involves three critical groups: dedicated educators (principals and teachers), involved parents, and motivated children. As a principal, you know that you and your teachers are dedicated to the education enterprise and trained to teach and motivate your students while they're in your care. But the students are only in your building 15% of the time *at best*. "How can I get parents more involved in their children's education?" has to be one of the most frequently asked questions whenever educators get together. Based on both our own experience and our observations of schools that are effectively involving parents in school activities, we believe it's not as difficult as it sometimes seems. However, the degree of difficulty is inevitably higher when we're working parents of low socioeconomic status (SES).

THE IMPORTANCE OF PARENT INVOLVEMENT

We all recognize that most children benefit from having parents actively involved in their education, and for children from low-income homes, parent involvement can be the single most important factor in fostering cognitive and emotional resilience in the face of multiple stressors (Garmezy, 1991; Myers & Taylor, 1998). The Head Start program is a prime illustration of the success of this involvement. Since its implementation in the 1960s, Head Start has grown into the largest federally funded program dedicated solely to promoting school readiness. One major component in the Head Start program is the parent-to-program connection. Imbedded in the Head Start program, this formalized system of parent involvement gives parents numerous opportunities to come into the classroom and participate in the curriculum, view children's growth and work products, and interact with faculty and staff. This involvement by parents is expected, and the measures set in place to ensure it occurs are critical to children's success because they reduce the discontinuity between the home and school environments and establish early expectations for *both* the home and the child.

This early connection between homes and schools promotes success on several levels. Those of you who work in Title I schools know that regular interaction with parents nurtures a trusting relationship between you and the parents. It also enables you to get firsthand knowledge of the sociocultural environments of your students. This not only allows you to put in place a curriculum that capitalizes on the strengths of your students and addresses their weaknesses but also gives you the opportunity to demonstrate appropriate educational interactions with children that parents can transfer to the home. Parent involvement serves to promote children's adaptation to school and significantly reduces behavior problems and school failure (Alexander & Entwisle, 1988). Furthermore, children whose parents are involved in the school have higher attendance rates, develop more positive attitudes toward school, exhibit more positive behaviors, and experience better interactions with peers (Koonce & Harper, 2005). Involved parents show their children that education isn't about just the curriculum but also the family and community.

Parent involvement is usually defined in school-centered terms such as how many times parents attend conferences or volunteer in the classroom. In addition, we hope to see parents participating in science fairs, cultural nights, concerts, conferences, and PTA meetings and volunteering as room mothers and fathers. This type of involvement is notably higher among parents from higher socioeconomic environments for various reasons. While we value this latter type of parent participation, there's evidence that it may have very little impact on a child's academic success because there's usually very limited contact between parent and child during these times (Ritblatt, Beatty, Cronan, &

Ochoa, 2002). While we all want parent involvement in our classrooms, most of our teachers have had little if any training in strategies for working collaboratively with families (Burton, 1992; Epstein, 1992). Teachers are trained to promote the growth and development of children, not parents (Cullingford & Morrison, 1999). Since we need involved parents, we may need to coach teachers concerning how to work as effectively as possible with them.

THE IMPORTANCE OF HOME-BASED INVOLVEMENT

Parents' involvement in their children's education doesn't happen only at school. Home-based involvement by parents may be more closely linked with academic success, and yet, unless we are in close communication with parents, we can't be sure students are getting the educational support they need. Parents who are involved on the home front are those who read to their children, help them with their homework, talk with them about academic issues such as the choices for science projects and performances on tests, and create a quiet place for their children to study. This kind of parent involvement appears to have a greater impact on academic success than school-based involvement. That's not to say, however, that school-based involvement is not valuable. It's generally through school-based interactions that parents learn ways to help their children at home, both through discussions with their children's teachers or other parents and by observing their own children in the classroom environment.

Sometimes, it's easier to lament the lack of parent involvement in low-income schools than to reflectively analyze and accommodate the reasons for their lack of involvement. Many low SES parents face serious time constraints related to their work hours. In addition, parents' perceptions of the teachers' attitudes toward them and their circumstances can significantly affect their willingness to come to school and into the classroom. Self-consciousness about their level of education, command of the English language, or ability to pay for school supplies and proper clothing can also deter parents from coming to school. When we have a clear understanding of the consequences of poverty and the limitations it places on parents' involvement, acknowledge that most parents—regardless of income—want to be there for their children, and consider ourselves coteachers with parents, we'll take a huge step toward establishing a school culture in which low SES parents feel welcome to participate.

To establish and pursue the goal of creating a school culture that's welcoming to all, we must ensure that all parties involved in a child's education are present, validated, and actively engaged. As with any good design for success, we can't achieve exceptional education if one of the parties is missing.

Unfortunately, in too many schools, the best we've been able to come up with as far as inspiring parents to become active shareholders in their children's education is the periodic parent-teacher conference and the occasional newsletter sent home. As we all know, this isn't working. If it was working, the lack of parent involvement wouldn't be the hot topic in every staff meeting, regional conference, and school board list of goals. The problem with our previous attempts to engage parents in the educational arena is that we've been pulling and tugging at them rather than *inviting* them.

How do we get parents to become our partners in their children's education? How do we get them to come to us, inquire about and become excited about the avenues open to them for participation? We might look at how government entities, businesses, and even the military have changed the way they attract their participants. They've all started to respond to changing demographics and altered their approaches to doing business to appeal to the interests and needs of their changing publics. We educators, for all our championing of thinking "outside of the box" and higher-level processing skills, have remained mired in doing things "the way we've always done them." We contend that the climate we create in our schools, the effectiveness with which we work within a multicultural community, and the way we manage our interactions with parents provide real opportunities to create strong school-home relationships.

THE IMPORTANCE OF SCHOOL CLIMATE

The well-known Canadian thinker Marshall McCluhan coined the phrase "the medium is the message" to illustrate that everything that surrounds a message strongly influences how we perceive it. What message do low SES parents get when they first enter your building? What does your school tell them about the people who work there? Do they feel welcome? In how many languages are the direction signs in the main lobby written? Do faculty and staff acknowledge visitors before they seek recognition? If you were a low SES parent who was already confused by cultural differences or feeling powerless in dealing with poverty, it wouldn't take much to discourage you from visiting your child's school. One disdainful look at your clothing, one sarcastic response to a question you asked, one impatient reminder of the correct protocol for visiting the building, being overlooked—just once—as you stood in the office with people you view as being of a higher economic or social status than yourself would surely be enough to send you scurrying.

How do we create a positive, welcoming school climate? One of the principals we observed said, "It's not complicated. Just think of your school as your home and consider how you treat your personal guests. When you have that picture in your mind, transfer it to your building or your classroom. Look around and see what would make the building or room more welcoming, more gracious, more comfortable for your guests." Below, we share a couple of examples from the effective schools we observed.

When one new principal first walked into her school, she was immediately struck by the deli-style counter that divided the lobby in half. It was customary for parents to come up to the counter to be "served." Three secretaries sat behind the counter, and the assistant principal's and principal's offices were behind them and out of sight. Responding to her own sense of apprehension when she entered the office, she asked the custodians if the counter was fastened to the floor or could be removed. Her administrative assistant was appalled. "If you take that counter out, people will just march in. They'll just walk up to your office to see you. We deal with some rough folks around here. That's not a good idea." The principal politely asked, "Do we also deal with very nice people?" One of the secretaries replied, "Oh yes, we have some very nice parents." "Well," replied the principal, "let's welcome them all and maybe the more intimidating ones will follow suit." The principal had the counter removed. It was a simple and practically cost-free change that made every visitor to the office feel welcome and important.

Another of the schools we observed served a population with a wide range of ethnic backgrounds and socioeconomic levels. Children were bussed in from a large geographical area, and many parents had no idea where many of the students in the school lived or played. The children shared little in the way of extracurricular activities and tended to hold stereotypical ideas about what "the others" do in their neighborhoods. To bridge the cultural gaps and create a clearer sense of community and shared values, the staff obtained, for free, an old television from the district warehouse and installed it prominently in the main lobby where parents generally waited for their children at the end of the day or when picking them up for a doctor's appointment. They connected a donated laptop computer to the TV and created a computer slide show that continuously displayed pictures of the school's students engaged in both curricular and extracurricular activities. They encouraged parents to contribute pictures to the slide show to supplement those taken by teachers who were attending, and had photographed, Little League games, karate lessons, dance recitals, track meets, and other events. The parents loved it and were often observed sharing stories about their children as they watched the pictures click by. The financial cost to the school was minimal; the cultural understanding gains to the school community—immeasurable!

Setting the Right Example

When there are problems, it's not unusual to hear a principal lament, "The buck *stops* here." What we often forget is that good things must also *start* with the principal. We must work to eliminate the elitist attitude that the school has the ultimate knowledge and authority (Cullingford & Morrison,

1999). We must be the ophthalmologists who craft the right lenses through which our faculties and staffs view our communities. We need to model for our education team how to welcome parents and community members as valuable partners in the education endeavor.

The days are long gone when the primary job of the principal was to simply manage a facility. Today, to lead the education process successfully, principals need an open door. To us, an open door means an open office, open mind, and open lines of communication. Every parent in your school, and especially low SES parents, needs to have a means to communicate with you easily.

We clearly have a wide variety of communication tools available, but the most sophisticated tool in your toolbox is your own sense of urgency about the communications you receive. E-mails, phone messages, and questions in the front lobby can't wait days or weeks to be answered. When parents walk up to your door and say, "I'm sorry to bother you," your response must be quick and warm. The pen you're pushing across that work order or the evaluation you're typing is never as important as the concern that brought these parents to your door. If you dismiss them or direct them to the front desk to make an appointment, you'll rob yourself of the opportunity to learn important information about your students and your community. You need to know that a family is splitting up or being evicted, that a second grader is being bullied on the bus and is afraid to come to school, that a mom needs help filling out a free or reduced lunch form, or that a nervous kindergarten mom needs reassurance as she cries over leaving her firstborn alone with you all day for the first time. The principal in one of the schools we observed had tacked a sign over her office door that said, "Remember the mission, not your position" to remind herself that whoever or whatever came through that door was in her job description.

We can't afford to isolate ourselves from the communities we serve. Some of our most effective principals have come up with creative ways to reach out to their communities. Among the techniques the principals we observed used were the following:

- Rode a school bus home with the kids every once in a while and, as the children got off the bus, greeted the waiting parents.
- Hosted a "Mom's Muffins" or "Dad's Doughnuts" every quarter to set time aside to talk to parents.
- Showed up at a neighborhood Little League game periodically to cheer for the local teams.
- Picked up a folder from their administrative assistants every day as they left that contained all the paperwork they needed to complete (signing checks, purchase orders, work orders, pieces of mail that arrived that day and needed attention) and dealt with all of it at home each night. "Not one of these tasks was worth missing a minute with my kids," one told us emphatically.

- Gave parents their direct school or cell telephone numbers and told the community it's okay to call whenever they have a serious concern, no matter the time of day.
- Established one day every week as "Dining with Dads" and another day as "Meals with Moms" so that parents who work late at night can rest and then come join their children for lunch. Not only does it give parents and children, who sometimes don't see much of each other, a time to connect, it can also give you valuable time to interact with parents.

As principal, the job of developing a school-home community of educators is yours. The principalship is not about power and prestige; it's about *community* education. It's okay for you to teach afterschool clubs, play jacks with kids on the floor, make home visits, call to see how a new mother is doing, go to the local neighborhood center to visit, take calculated risks when the odds are in your favor that the outcome will be more beneficial than what the norm is producing, admit you don't know all the answers, and ask your teachers for help. It's only when we humanize ourselves that we can have those serious conversations with parents about their responsibility for their children's attendance; firmly walk a hovering parent out the door on the first day of school; ask those difficult questions so we're all on the same team when family issues or financial problems arise; speak directly, honestly, and openly with parents about their child with special needs without the parents taking offense; or give parents suggestions about behavior management at home that may change behavior at school in a nonadversarial way. Max DuPree, the former CEO of Herman Miller, the furniture manufacturer, said it best: "The only thing the world believes is behavior, because we all see it instantaneously. None of us may preach anymore. We must behave!" (Dupree, 1989, p. 89).

Making the Parent-Friendly Climate Pervasive

The parent-friendly climate of your school can't be limited to your accessibility and responsiveness alone. Everyone who works in your school, including teachers, counselors, aides, office personnel, custodians, and food service workers, has to demonstrate the same quality of welcoming behavior and reinforce the concept of the shared school-home responsibility for children's education and well-being. As principal, it's your job to communicate clearly and specifically your expectations for how parents and other guests are to be greeted and responded to, monitor faculty and staff behavior continuously, and recognize, reward, and reinforce appropriate friendly responsiveness routinely.

As educators, we all recognize that one of the unfortunate realities of our schools today is the need for unprecedented security measures. While it's awful to think that we need to protect our children from people who would do them harm, in fact, we must. How do we maintain necessary security procedures and still create and maintain a welcoming school climate? First, we remember that parents have entrusted their children to our care and expect us to keep them safe. Second, we remember the indignities of poorly handled or seemingly "profiled" security checks that many of us have endured since September 11, 2001, and vow not to inflict them on guests in our schools.

Requests for proof of identification don't have to be delivered with hard-eyed police-state precision. Such requests can easily be accompanied by a smile and couched in a friendly explanation of why it's necessary to the safety of the students for the school to be sure of the identity of visitors. Office staff should be well informed about alternative forms of identification that are acceptable and the importance of patience in helping parents understand their options. Parents and other guests who have a legitimate reason to be in the building should always be politely and cheerfully escorted to the appropriate classroom and introduced or presented to the teacher or counselor. When handled with friendliness and respect, the school's security procedures will reassure, rather than deter, parents.

MEETING THE CHALLENGES PRESENTED BY LOW SES NEIGHBORHOODS

In schools in low SES neighborhoods, one factor that often seems to present the toughest challenge—cultural differences—can be the easiest and most rewarding to overcome. To do so requires a proactive approach to recognize the number of different cultures your students represent and how this may affect the attitudes of parents and their aptitude for participation. While all of our parents are united in their love for their children and a desire to provide their children with the best possible education, their understanding of the education process and how they can become actively involved may vary greatly.

A significant majority of low SES students live in low-income neighborhoods. It's unfortunate but true that low-income neighborhoods tend to be home to large populations of Black, Hispanic, and recent immigrant families. As a result, schools that serve large numbers of low SES students tend to be more multicultural than schools in higher-income neighborhoods. If you work in such schools and want to establish and maintain strong school-home relationships, you need to create an environment that embraces all cultures and work proactively to identify and mitigate cultural factors that challenge the development of those relationships.

Parents who enjoy a higher standard of living generally share the prevailing culture of the neighborhood school and are comfortable participating in the activities most valued by the school culture or most likely to promote their children's academic success. Their family and work situations tend to permit involvement at school during the regular school day. This makes it easier for them to establish effective lines of communication with faculty and staff than for parents of low SES children. As we mentioned before, low SES parents may not have the flexible work schedules, child care options, or access to transportation to become as fully involved in their children's schools. Even when they can get to the schools, low SES parents may have little understanding of the questions they should ask the teacher, how to act in a classroom, or how to build a collegial partnership with a teacher (Lott, 2001).

If they don't feel a part of the school culture, low SES parents may encounter several problems. They may be less likely to receive the social, informational, or material rewards enjoyed by those parents who have more visibility with faculty and staff. They may also be viewed as uncaring by school faculty and staff, and this perception can have negative outcomes for their children when internalized by their classroom teachers. According to Hill and Craft (2003), when teachers perceive involved parents as valuing education, this perception is often translated into higher teacher rating of student work. To us, this means that when low SES parents aren't actively involved in the school, teachers' deficit perception can negatively affect their attitudes toward the low SES students' abilities and work products.

As principals, it's our responsibility to set a tone that encourages parents to get involved and provide a culture in which their willingness to participate can come to fruition. If we don't enable these parents to join the school culture, they won't feel welcome and we'll miss the opportunity to build the school-home partnership that can enhance their children's educational success.

Overcoming Time and Transportation Challenges

If we want low SES parents to participate in school-sponsored activities, we have to schedule those activities at a time that works with their schedules. How can we bemoan their lack of participation in PTA meetings, for example, when we convene them at a time when these parents are working or in the evening when they'd have to find babysitters for their children?

Unless they live very close to the school, most students travel to and from school by bus. Their parents are not so well served. In many low SES homes, personal transportation options are limited. Low-income parents may need to take a bus to the doctor's office or the grocery store. Their everyday errands can require twice as much time as those of parents who have operating vehicles at their disposal. These same parents must rely on public transportation, and its attendant cost and scheduling problems, to get to school-related events.

The principals we observed placed accessibility at the forefront when planning school activities. Some held PTA meetings scheduled early in the school year at local neighborhood centers to make it easier for low SES parents to attend. While their primary goal was to bring the parents into the school environment, they pointed out that these neighborhood meetings served to "break the ice" and get the conversation, and the relationships, started. These meetings also provided parents the opportunity to meet other parents who might be able to provide transportation to future meetings held at the school or suggest older children who could serve as babysitters. Some other initiatives these principals undertook to enable low SES parents to come to school events included

- ensuring that all teachers had information concerning their student's siblings in the school so they could collaborate with the siblings' teachers to schedule parent-teacher conferences for the families in a convenient block of time;
- giving the parents options regarding the timing of parent-teacher conferences, including early morning, Saturday, and evening hours;
- providing parents in low-income-housing neighborhoods a list of school families who resided within their own neighborhoods, so carpooling could be arranged;
- arranging with a local church attended by many of the school's families to transport parents from a church location to scheduled school events in the church van;
- permitting counselors, administrators, and parent liaisons to pick up and return parents who wanted to come to school to volunteer, have lunch with their children, or attend a teacher conference; and
- asking the PTA for a "Taxi Fund" to be used in true emergencies to transport parents to the school.

Overcoming the Lack of Education Resources in Low SES Homes

In Chapter 3, we identified some common disconnects that can occur between teachers' expectations regarding the home environment of low SES students and the realities of those homes. One of the most common disconnects involves the education resources available in low SES homes. Whether we're talking about the amount of time low SES parents can spend helping their children with homework or the availability of material resources like books, art supplies, work space, computers, and Internet access, low SES home resources too frequently fall short of teachers' general expectations. The principals and teachers in the schools we observed worked to overcome this challenge in two basic ways. First, they adjusted their teaching methods and assignments to accommodate the situation; second, they found ways to make needed resources more readily available to low SES students.

Recognizing that many low SES parents may not have either the time or the ability to ensure their children complete their homework assignments, a number of the teachers set aside time at the end of the school day for students to begin their assignments. In doing so, they were able to answer students' questions and make sure they would be able to complete the work on their own. They also limited the amount of homework they required. Their thinking was that if their students can do 5 math problems correctly, they don't need to do 20 more.

To accommodate the lack of education resources in the homes of the low SES students, most of the schools we observed instituted afterschool homework clubs and curriculum-connected clubs in which they taught chess, sewing, cooking, art, photography, creative writing, and so on. The main objective of these activities was to reinforce basic learning skills in a fun way.

To make sure that low SES students had the school supplies they needed at the beginning of the school year, the principals and counselors in several schools actively solicited supplies from churches, businesses, and civic organizations that routinely run such programs. One school in our study used a commercial company to fill school supply lists. Any parent who wished to do so could purchase a school supply box for their child, and it would be ready for pick up the first day of school. To ensure that there would be enough supply boxes for the low SES students, the principal sent a letter to all parents asking those who could afford it to donate one additional supply box. Happily, they reported that, each September, every child receives a supply box.

Technology is a fast-changing field and what's new today may be passé next week. In several of the low-income schools we observed, teachers, principals, and PTA members routinely approached businesses in which computer hardware, software, and peripherals were regularly replaced (banks, hospitals, universities, hi-tech business such as phone companies, healthcare facilities, insurance agents, and so on all discard their used equipment) and offered to take any equipment they were discarding and distribute it to needy homes.

Another school we observed conducted widely publicized annual children's book drives and used grants from organizations like Phi Delta Kappa to purchase books to be distributed to students. During the May kindergarten orientation, when all prospective five-year-olds come to visit the school and parents are given an overview of the school, immunizations needed, and school policies, they present every kindergartener with three picture books. At the end of the year, the school gives every student two books to keep and read over the summer. These books are leveled just above the students' reading level to encourage new learning over the summer and deter some loss of skills while the children are on vacation.

Dealing Effectively With Language Limitations

As we're all aware, low-income neighborhoods tend to be home to many immigrant populations in which English is not the first language. While children tend to learn conversational English fairly quickly through interactions with their peers and school experiences, their parents are often much slower to develop a working understanding of it. And, it's not only the immigrant populations that have trouble understanding school-oriented communication. For example, the "Schoolese" we educators speak may be as confusing as a foreign language to even native-born parents. It's futile to speak about benchmarks, assessments, curriculum pacing, frameworks, and No Child Left Behind, or use all those strange acronyms with parents who lack adequate formal education or facility with English. Acronyms, we believe, should never appear in any school-home communications.

It's equally meaningless to send home important communications that aren't translated into the languages the parents best understand. If we don't, how can we complain that several Hispanic parents dropped their children off at school on a teacher workday if the announcement of the school holiday they received wasn't translated into Spanish? It's our job to communicate our message in a way parents can accurately receive it.

We recommend that schools in which 15% or more of the students represent a particular ethnicity translate an equal percentage of all school-home communication materials into that language and have at least one speaker of that culture's language present during school hours to translate and interpret conversations between teachers, parents, and students. Where can you find translators and interpreters? Principals we've observed find them among the parents, through local churches and cultural centers, and among students at local colleges and universities—volunteers! And don't forget the community-service credits that some high schools offer their students. Some of your former students might be proud and willing to help you in this way.

Developing Effective Lines of Communication

A key element in communication is the quality of the relationship between the message sender and the message receiver. The more comfortable the communicators are with each other, the more effective their communication is. While the bookshelves of the world are full of books detailing the intricacies of interpersonal communication, we see the development of effective communication between school faculty and staff and students' parents as a simple common-sense process. In general, we communicate more easily with people who speak our own language. We exchange information more successfully with people we know, like, trust, and respect. We communicate more effectively with those we view as our peers than with those we view as our "superiors," and we communicate more efficiently when we share the same background information about the subject under discussion as the people we're talking to.

We believe the first step in developing effective lines of school-home communication is making it easy for parents to get to know, like, trust, and respect us—to see us as their peers, not their superiors. This is especially important when working with low SES parents. In the schools we observed, every parent or visitor to the school was greeted with a warm smile and a personal—not "professional"—introduction like "Good morning, my name is Phyllis Jones. I'm the office secretary. How can I help you?" Every parent was introduced by name to everyone they encountered. "Mrs. Martinez, this is Mary Smith, the school nurse," or, "Mrs. Martinez, this is Susan Wilson, Juan's teacher. Susan, this is Mrs. Martinez, Juan's mother." The principals in these schools introduced themselves to parents not as Dr. So-and-so but by their first and last names. The message this sends—and it's a powerful one— is we're happy to see you, and we're ready, willing, and able to help you solve whatever problem brought you here.

To develop parents' trust and respect, the faculty and staff of the schools we observed communicated with parents in honest, candid terms. They shared good news and bad news with parents. When they had a problem to report, they accompanied it with suggestions for ways to resolve the problem. And they took a proactive approach to making sure that parents had the information they needed. We mentioned earlier the value of translating written communications into the languages parents read most effectively and in having interpreters available when needed. Even if a second meeting has to be scheduled at a time when an interpreter will be available to facilitate the conversation, the clear message to the parent is that we're interested enough in your child and you to spend the time necessary to ensure mutual understanding.

One of the best ways to develop lines of communication with parents is to make sure they have as much information about the school and its programs as possible. Back-to-school letters are valuable tools to start this process. The principal's back-to-school letter should first and foremost be inviting and include clear statements of the overall school policies, schedules, and so on, and information about the special programs available, with clear instructions concerning application processes and deadlines. In the schools we observed, the teachers also sent back-to-school letters to parents. These invited and welcomed the family into the school culture and clearly outlined classroom routines, schedules, and homework and discipline policies.

A number of the teachers we observed also sent one-page newsletters to parents, once or twice a month, to keep parents informed about the curriculum content being taught, upcoming events and projects, timelines, field trips, class rules, and school holidays. Some included photos of the students and samples of student writing as well. These teachers felt the effort was worthwhile because parents reported that the newsletter helped them better understand the classroom environment. These newsletters always included a phone number or e-mail address parents could use to keep in touch with the teacher and asked parents to share a work phone number the teachers could use to contact them if necessary. Other teachers made once-a-month phone calls to the parents of all their students to maintain a routine school-home connection. They noted this was an effective way to build trust and make it easier to enlist a parent's help if a problem developed.

One school we observed makes a curriculum call to every student's home every two weeks by using a system that disaggregates the students by grade level and automatically calls the phone number in the data base system with a recorded message concerning the children's classes; for example,

> Good afternoon, this is Jean Jones, principal at Elmwood School. Your third grader is learning about direction this week. The words she or he is using are, *north, south, east,* and *west.* If you have maps in your home or car, ask your child to find a city and tell you the direction you must travel to reach that destination. Have a great week, and thank you for helping us teach your child.

Not only does this give parents an idea about what their children are learning but it also identifies a way in which they can promote that learning.

The principals and teachers we observed also visited parents in their homes. They see home visits as an extension of their willingness to meet and talk with parents about ways to help their children succeed in school. They noted that they exercised caution when venturing into some neighborhoods. Several noted that they had established a buddy system for visits into high-crime neighborhoods, and they never visited a home without making an appointment. The reward for this extra effort on the teachers' part was to establish contact with parents and make it easier for parents to participate in a productive relationship with the school.

One of the best communication channels available to us as educators is parents who are already active in school events. While they're often effective in their "over the backyard fence" conversations, there may be an even better way to use their talents. Does your school have a parent center that's set up for parent volunteers? If we believe that parents are an integral factor in their children's education, then allotting space for them in the school is a gesture that speaks volumes about the welcome we're extending. Parents can mentor each other about the ins and outs of the school better than any teacher or principal— if the environment is provided. A school-based center gives parents a place to communicate with and learn from other parents; it's a forum in which they can socialize and learn about upcoming events, enrichment activities, parenting tips, how to help with homework, and how to access resources. They can share educational and behavioral expectations and develop common approaches to handling misbehaviors in their neighborhoods. The more comfortable parents are in the school building with us, the better we're able to work with them on behalf of their children's education.

EMBRACING CULTURAL DIVERSITY

Although demographic studies predict that the White, non-Hispanic majority in our country is likely to become the minority population in the next quarter century, the culture of most of our public schools is still predominantly White. This can make it uncomfortable for recent immigrant parents to participate in school activities. And, sometimes it's parents' perceptions of our role as educators that hamper their participation. For instance, in many Hispanic households teachers and principals are viewed as the knowledgeable leaders for education, and parents believe all they need do is take their children to school, and the educators will do the rest. Because this cultural perception isn't widely discussed, it can easily be misunderstood as lack of parent interest. If we want parents involved in their children's education, we need to communicate in every way possible that we value cultural diversity and believe it enriches our educational programs.

In this era of global communication and commerce, the more our children know about other cultures and languages, the better prepared they'll be to prosper as adults. While this is clear to us, it doesn't make it any more comfortable for the parents of some of our students to come into the school. In the schools we observed, both principals and teachers found many ways to communicate their appreciation of diverse cultures and invite parents into the education process. We think their good ideas can only inspire you to think of even more creative ways to make minority parents feel welcome in your building.

One of the principals we observed, seeking ways to enhance students' appreciation of their own and others' cultures, took the opportunity at a PTA meeting to ask a parent to come to school and read to her daughter's class. The parent was immediately embarrassed and explained that she couldn't read in English, only in Spanish. The principal responded that it would be a welcome opportunity for the class to hear a book read in a different language and that the non-Spanish-speaking children would understand the story through the pictures. Subsequently, this parent went to school at least once every quarter to read a Spanish-language children's book, to the delight of all. Another principal, recognizing the role that food plays in many traditional cultures, instituted "International Nights" to which each family is asked to bring a dish that represents their own culture. He commented that the food was delicious and the events proved to be excellent opportunities to exchange information with parents.

Other examples of how the schools we observed embraced the cultural beliefs of their students and their families include

- providing Muslim children a quiet and secure place to spend lunch periods when they are celebrating holidays such as Ramadan that require fasting;
- recognizing the appropriateness of children of the Russian Orthodox faith to stay home from school to celebrate the Russian Orthodox Christmas, which comes later than our standard winter break;
- allowing a child to read in the library instead of attending a music class that is in conflict with her religious beliefs;
- celebrating the winter holidays of all faiths by decorating the school lobby with a Christmas tree, Hanukah menorah, Kwanzaa tables, and depictions of Middle Eastern holidays, and holding an all-school party featuring the symbols of each;
- inviting parents to suggest music representative of their cultures for school concerts; and
- staging an "International Exposition" in the school, featuring articles of cultural clothing, jewelry, relics, pictures, and so on that parents bring in to showcase.

These are just a few examples of ways in which cultural boundaries can be blurred and promote the ideas that, regardless of our heritage or financial situations, we're all equally engaged in the education process, and parents' involvement is welcomed and crucial to our success. Recognizing and welcoming the cultural differences among the parents of your students makes it easier for them to work with you and you with them.

SUMMARY

Education researchers tell us, and we know from our own experience, that children do better in school when their parents are actively involved in the education process. We also know from experience that, for low SES children, parent involvement in their education can be difficult to cultivate but wonderful to achieve. We welcome the challenge of reaching out to these parents and inviting them into our schools, and we know there are many avenues available to reach this goal if we're committed to succeeding. We also observed that low SES parents' feelings of connectedness and worth resulted in their increased involvement in the schools we studied.

5 How Strong School- Business Relationships Can Benefit Low SES Students

Through conversations with local business leaders, we've learned that one byproduct of the No Child Left Behind (NCLB) Act is the negative message delivered to the business sector that public education, as a system, is failing. While not necessarily a new complaint, since the advent of NCLB publicity, it's not uncommon for us to hear business people say, "Kids today are coming out of school without the skills to do the job!" While NCLB reports of failing schools have added fuel to the complaints voiced by business people, we strongly believe that NCLB might be one of the important reasons why students are not developing the higher-level thinking skills that businesses look for. It's apparent to us that, to meet NCLB requirements, low-performing students are frequently taught by the rote memorization method with only one objective in mind—passing the state standardized tests.

We suggest that, for our business communities to get an accurate picture of the good learning that's actually taking place in our schools, we must work with local businesses as partners, not adversaries. We can help businesses understand that even when student scores meet the state-mandated standards, such scores don't necessarily translate into students having the higher-level thinking skills they're seeking. We need to work together with our business community toward a common goal of producing students who are strong communicators, high-level critical thinkers, and effective problem solvers.

To us, learning about how the business world works, while teaching business about the work we do as educators, offers benefits for both enterprises and provides resources that would otherwise be unavailable to our low socioeconomic status (SES) students. We see three fundamental requirements for developing strong school-business relationships:

1. Creating a partnership with structure and reciprocity

2. Looking beyond dollars at the role of school-business partnerships

3. Recognizing the partnership value of small local businesses

CREATING A PARTNERSHIP WITH STRUCTURE AND RECIPROCITY

If a school-business partnership is to begin with a high probability of success, both the school and the business must have clearly defined goals, a mutual understanding of the contributions expected of each party, and people and processes in place to manage the operations. In the schools we observed, the principals initiated the business partnerships and maintained a lead role in their development and management.

The Principal's Role

The principals we observed understood that embarking on a partnership with business means venturing into a different culture, and they recognized the need to make themselves familiar with the business culture and develop strategies to work successfully within it. Among the strategies they found successful in approaching the business community and developing productive relationships are the following:

- Learn as much as you can about the businesses in your school community that might be viable partners if approached. If you're able to, visit their websites and take note of their products, services, and achievements. Your ability to demonstrate your interest in and knowledge of their enterprises will promote their interest in yours.
- Explore whether you share any mutual contacts. Perhaps a staff member knows someone employed at a particular business, or another of your

business partners has had dealings with them. Networking to gain an introduction to the business is far more productive than making a cold call. Your business people will readily attest to that fact.

- Make appointments with potential business partners for face-to-face meetings. At any such meetings, start by communicating your school's vision for your students. Don't begin your conversations with a list of wants. Take time to let potential business partners identify ways they might be able to become partners in your school's vision and any specific efforts to achieve that vision.

- Invite representatives from potential business partners to visit your school. Becoming familiar with your school's philosophy and operations may help them generate ideas about ways they can contribute.

- Identify the resources your school is willing to commit to any partnership. Businesses are used to planning and developing goal-oriented projects. They need to understand and appreciate your commitment to any partnership agenda.

- Highlight the potential benefits businesses will receive as a result of a partnership. Good public relations is as important to business as it is to your school.

- Communicate clearly how the business's contributions will benefit your students at every opportunity. Businesses operate on the basis of results, so be as specific as possible.

- Join your local Chamber of Commerce. Put yourself in a position to meet and talk with other business people on their "turf" about all the positive things your school is doing. You never know when you may spark interest in an otherwise disinterested business leader.

- Be on the lookout for new businesses trying to establish themselves in your neighborhood. Businesses need to know that your parents, students, faculty, and staff constitute an important potential customer base and that you have regular lines of communication with them.

The Role of the Business Partnership Coordinator

Recognizing that business leaders, like you, probably can't commit full-time effort to a school-business partnership, the principals we observed generally assigned a coordinator to serve as the key communicator with their business partners to ensure that agreed upon goals and expectations are realized, reciprocity is maintained, and communication is continuous. Since few schools can afford to hire such a person, the principals we observed found ways to provide some released time for a faculty or staff member, or identified a community patron or parent, willing and able to volunteer as the school's business partnership coordinator. These principals all noted that designating a business partnership coordinator requires as much thought and attention as hiring a new teacher because the coordinator can make or break existing partnerships and promote or destroy future possibilities. When thinking about an ideal business partnership coordinator for your school, think effervescent salesperson and marketing expert with solid organizational skills and a track record for follow-through.

In general, and in addition to recruiting new business partners, the role of the business partnership coordinator is to ensure the following:

- That the communication links with all partner businesses are established early and maintained throughout the year. In addition to project-specific communications, it's a good plan to routinely send school newsletters and announcements about PTA meetings, school picnics, assemblies, field trips, and so on, and provide business partners with access to your school's website, on which you always list, and often feature, your school's business partners in an extremely positive light.
- That, whenever possible, media events are arranged and coordinated that highlight the workings and results of the partnership program and the contributions of all your business partners. Public recognition is a very effective way to foster sustained partnerships. An invitation to a quarterly breakfast or a Cub Scout banquet at your school, for example, can provide substance to your promise of reciprocity.

LOOKING BEYOND DOLLARS IN SCHOOL-BUSINESS PARTNERSHIPS

In these economically challenging times of budget cuts, reduced tax bases, and high energy costs, it's natural to seek out business partnerships that can provide some financial resources to your school. We'd all like a business partner like Intel, which spends about $120 million a year to promote technology in schools. However, a sure way to scare off a potential business partner is to start any conversation by requesting money. It's much more beneficial to begin a business relationship based on recognition of potential mutual interests and how reciprocal advantages can be enjoyed by both parties. In the schools we observed, the principals reported that the feelings expressed by both school and business leaders about their partnerships focus on the pride, fulfillment, and sense of community the partnerships produce.

Of course, it would be wonderful if we could all find business partners willing and able to contribute financial capital to our schools. On the other hand, there are many opportunities for business partnerships to add to the educational capital of a school that don't deal with direct transfers of dollars and are extremely beneficial in schools that serve low-income neighborhoods. Some of the ways that local business partners contributed in the low-income neighborhoods of the schools we observed included the following:

- Providing reading buddies to work with kindergartners entering school without the necessary prerequisite skills intact, by giving employees an hour away from work without losing pay
- Providing mentoring for young children from low SES homes who lacked consistency of an adult presence
- Supervising and assisting at an afterschool homework club for young children who would otherwise have to do their homework without an adult to assist them or in an unstructured environment at home
- Hosting a free Tax Preparation Night at school for families who can't afford professional tax preparation and providing a Spanish-speaking counselor to ensure Spanish-speaking parents understand complicated tax laws and codes
- Sponsoring a running club to promote fitness with a low-income population prone to diabetes, obesity, and asthma
- Volunteering to spend two nights each school quarter to help parents become more sophisticated with computer technology and learn how to monitor their children's access
- Providing refreshments for teacher workdays, parent teas, and school picnics
- Donating gift certificates for a principal to use as raffle prizes at staff meetings
- Sponsoring an event that gives students the opportunity to shadow a business employee
- Sponsoring summer internships for students seriously interested in pursuing a career in the business partner's field

These examples demonstrate ways that business partners can provide valuable services and expertise that are of special benefit to low SES students and their families at minimal cost.

RECOGNIZING THE PARTNERSHIP VALUE OF SMALL LOCAL BUSINESSES

Many, if not most, of our low-income school communities don't include huge conglomerates and multimillion dollar corporations. One of the principals we observed told us that when she first started at her current school, she was told that business partnerships weren't possible because most of the stores, fast-food chains, and gas stations in the area were small and independently owned, with few employees, many of whom didn't speak fluent English. Several other principals we observed faced similar challenges in developing productive business partnerships in their attendance areas. However, recognizing that their student populations and families were all potential customers of their communities' "mom and pop" businesses, they understood that their students and those small business owners could mutually benefit each other. Among the school and small business partnerships we observed in action were the following:

- A landscaping business that worked with students after school to establish a butterfly garden and plant trees at the school site.
- An auto body shop that provided teachers with free yearly automobile inspections.
- A fast food operation that provided breakfast sandwiches for early-morning staff meetings.
- The owner and chef of a local ethnic restaurant who started a chef's club for interested students. He subsequently recruited other restaurant owners, and the members of the school's chef's club traveled each week to observe a different type of food being prepared.
- A construction company that purchased t-shirts for the school's softball team with the school's name partnered with the business's logo.
- A military unit that volunteered to supervise and assist at a biweekly homework club for students whose parents were stationed on the base.
- A homeowners' association that contributed money on an annual basis to support technology upgrades.

In every instance, the partnership contributed to the success of low SES students in return for public recognition of their business partnership activities. At the same time, every business was enlightened about the vast challenges and hard work taking place in their local school. One of the principals we observed developed an action plan for her particular business partnership program, which included the following two very important tenets:

1. School-business partnership actions and approaches had to be purposeful and initiated to fill a need within her school.

2. No business was to be solicited without a clear understanding of the specific need that could be filled or the way in which the school could specifically reciprocate.

SUMMARY

Just as government agencies and businesses have changed their ways of doing business due to changes in the marketplace, we must also alter the way we do business. As a principal, you need to be aware of the partnership opportunities available in your community and actively recruit business involvement in your school. Make your presence known in the entire community; ask neighborhood churches if you can leave your school's newsletter in the vestibule. Introduce yourself as the principal of your local school every time you make a purchase at a local store. Ask if you can place your newsletters on the grocery store bulletin board in at least two languages. And don't forget the local barbershops and beauty salons. Host an open house periodically for local businesses and take them on a tour of your school.

Efforts like these produce results. They're all tactics used by principals in our study to generate awareness of the school and its needs. Be proactive in your efforts, and let your imagination flow. Gone are the days when you can stand in your school's main entry area and expect that opportunity will knock on your door. You must court opportunity. As trite as it may sound, it does "take a village," but you may need to put the village together yourself.

6

The Role Networking Can Play in the Effective Education of Low SES Students

As we discussed in Chapter 5, it does indeed take a village, but what are the boundaries of your educational village? The principals of successful low socioeconomic schools we observed have become experts at building relationships not only with all support offices in their school districts but also with a wide-ranging network of resources that would otherwise go untapped.

The first step in broadening the field of shareholders in your school community is a very deliberate form of resource manipulation. We know, the word *manipulation* often congers up negative connotations of something that's perhaps unethical. Not so. Manipulation can be a positive action that produces positive results and injures no one, if done correctly. Successful manipulation of resources is an art, and it all begins with thoughtful and planned networking.

What we have discovered through interviews with resourceful principals is that the squeaky wheel *really is* the one that gets the grease. We believe that one of the first leadership strategies that should be pursued by all principals and taught to all preprincipal candidates is how to network for results.

NETWORKING WITH CENTRAL OFFICES

We know that each school district has a different configuration for its central offices. However, most school districts have assigned responsibility for special education, transportation, human resources, air and heat, warehouse storage, and building maintenance and repairs to specific administrators. Effective networking is not about the offices' titles or locations; it's about the dedicated people who make these operations run smoothly and can make or break your school. The principals we observed, who obtained positive results for their schools where others were unsuccessful, spent a considerable amount of time cultivating relationships with the people in their districts who control the resources. It wasn't unusual to find one of these principals visiting the maintenance shed with a tray of cookies or a box of donuts to say thank you for a job well done. All of the principals routinely called department heads to compliment crews that had worked in their buildings. They also made a special effort to welcome support personnel as they entered their buildings and thank them for their speedy response. They recognized that treating support personnel as fellow professionals and personally communicating their appreciation goes a long way toward ensuring consistent, positive responsiveness and performance.

Several of the principals we observed noted that they spend time calling district offices during the first week of school to reconnect with district officials. One of them took Thanksgiving dinner to the six security guards on duty to protect the schools over the holiday. No one was surprised by the courteous response and support her school always received when she called.

The savvy administrators we've come to know have also developed professional relationships with personnel in the human resources offices. They make personal visits to the staffing specialists' offices to discuss the philosophy of their school, school needs, and school climate, and reported that the resultant effective "resume matching" has benefited their schools numerous times. These principals told us that when their specialists receive a candidate's resume that has something they know a specific school is looking for, or when they recognize a potential match between a teacher and a particular school's philosophy, the referral is often right on target and culminates in a long-lasting teaching relationship in their school.

These principals also understood that when donations, grant opportunities, highly qualified resumes, extra furniture, and technology become unexpectedly available, it helps when your name, face, and needs are already in the minds of the powers that allocate. In addition to keeping in touch with central office people themselves, many of the principals we observed told us that when mentoring new assistant principals, they spend the first year introducing them to support office personnel and encouraging the assistant principals to form lasting relationships of their own.

NETWORKING BEYOND THE SCHOOL DISTRICT

Most of our successful principals believe their success at resource management is attributable to a history of well-planned, mutually beneficial personal relationships, as much as it's due to their academic expertise and leadership.

Your ability to successfully project a positive, professional image by speaking cordially and confidentially about your school's goals in face-to-face meetings, written communication, and appearances will result in valuable opportunities for your school. People have always developed professional networks over time, but with today's scarce resources, especially in low-socioeconomic areas, it's absolutely imperative that you systematically build relationships with professional friends and friends of those professionals in and out of your local school boundaries and the field of education.

An important factor to remember about networking is that it's actually about the other person. The best "networkers" make it all about other people. Their focus is always on making the other party feel respected, validated, and important. This can be a critical factor when you need another person's assistance. It's important to understand and remember that the last impression you made will guide their first reaction when you request their assistance.

Networking begins with having conversations and making meaningful contact with the people who come into your school—making everyone feel special. People generally have something they're thinking about and would love to talk to you about: their children, their jobs, or their hobbies. The people you meet will want to get to know you if they feel that you want to get to know them. It's human nature.

But networking doesn't happen only in your school or when you're visiting the central office. It happens all the time and everywhere: when you're at the grocery store, the bank, the dry cleaners, in your local barbershop or hair salon, at church or at a conference in another state. Don't miss an opportunity to speak about your school, its mission, and your needs. One of the principals we observed told us that, at a book signing at a local bookstore, she engaged in conversation with the person waiting next to her. After discussing the needs she had in a financially challenged neighborhood, the lady gave her a card and told her the next time she had a mother who needed a wardrobe so she could enter the job market to give her a call. The lady in line headed a nonprofit organization that did just that, helped women reenter the workplace. Had this principal chosen merely to wait in line, get her book signed, and leave, she would have missed a very positive networking opportunity.

Expanding the Reach of Your Network

There are valuable networks beyond your school system that will take time to ferret out. The principals who seem to get an edge on technology in their schools or find extra funds for playground equipment are those who search for opportunities to network. We aren't talking here about lasting partnerships as we did in Chapter 5, although such a partnership may form. Most networking involves casting a wide net to increase the number of individuals who know about your work, your school, and the school's vision, accomplishments, and needs.

One valuable resource in many areas is local homeowners' associations. A gentle reminder that property values are closely tied to the quality of the neighborhood schools resonates with most homeowners! Consider requesting a few minutes at scheduled meetings to inform property owners about the great things your school is doing and the needs you have.

Schools that serve low SES students need the support of middle- and upper-class homeowners. Unfortunately, too many of these families place their children in private schools, and it's the private sector that benefits from this resource. Everyone in your attendance area needs to hear from you, loud and clear, that, while you have challenges, your school offers an excellent education and is a safe, well-maintained community of learners. One of the schools we studied has seen, over a six-year period, a steady increase in the number of neighborhood children coming back to the neighborhood school even though nearly half of the students are bussed in from low-income housing and qualify for free and reduced lunches. This return has brought an increase in volunteers, fundraising, and partnerships, and a seed has been sown to unite the low-, middle-, and high-socioeconomic families in the school community.

These types of successes only result if you're willing to extend your reach to as many diverse groups as possible, for example, the Chamber of Commerce, local churches, daycare centers that your parents use, volunteer fire departments, Little League organizations, and community centers. The more people who know about you and your school, the more potential supporters you'll have.

We know it's not practical to think you can spend every day out on the road promoting your school. After all, there are children to educate! How well do you know the systems in which you operate? How familiar are you with the public relations mechanisms within your school district? Is there a medium for getting news out into the community about the great things you do in your school? The principals we observed have answered these questions and more, and freely use existing communication systems to work for the benefit of their schools.

One of the principals we observed appointed a public relations person on her staff who had majored in journalism before she became an educator. She made this individual responsible for identifying and promoting at least one positive school program, initiative, or activity every month. This in-house "PR person" regularly contacts the local newspapers, submits information to the school district's employee newsletter, and makes sure something new is always highlighted on the school marquee. The principal noted that a single mention in a countywide newspaper about an upcoming breakfast to celebrate Veteran's Day prompted a large city newspaper to send reporters to the school to do a story. That story brought volunteers to the school from the local Air Force base, and one of the volunteers procured barely used laptops for the school lab from a relative in the technology field. Well-placed information can produce a wide range of opportunities, if placed often, clearly, and in the right places.

Networking to Develop New Sources of Talent

As educators, we know there always seems to be a critical shortage of teachers, especially minority teachers, and especially in schools in low-socioeconomic neighborhoods. No school can be better than its teachers. The key to improving the education opportunities for the approximately 12 million children that come to us from poverty is to recruit the finest educators for them. As principals, we must use as many contacts as we can to locate and recruit the best teachers possible.

One thing we learned from our study is that too many teachers assigned to schools in low-income areas are not specifically trained to teach low SES children. To the extent that we can network with the education departments of local universities, we can lobby them to expand their curriculum to include course work to provide teachers with the skills, attitudes, and pedagogy required to teach low SES students successfully. In addition, we can take action to facilitate the process. Two of the principals we observed volunteered to host internships for education majors to help these budding teachers gain insight to the educational needs of low SES students. Not only did these internships benefit the education students but they also provided additional professional-level staff in the schools and gave the principals the opportunity to identify and recruit experienced teachers of observable promise.

You also need to become adept at networking outside the school district because selection is more important than training. The resumes of the best candidates may not be in your human resources offices, and the resumes you receive from human resources should not be the only resumes you seek. We recommend that you open dialogues with professors from your alma mater, colleagues in professional organizations such as the American Society for Curriculum Development, National Association of Elementary School Principals, and local education fraternities like Phi Delta Kappa and Kappa Delta Pi, focusing on the type of teachers you want in your school community. Such contacts can produce resumes you may never have had the opportunity to review otherwise.

While you can always provide staff development for a teacher who may not have all the educational skills, you can't develop empathy, devotion, and commitment in your teachers. The commitment to education demonstrated by the effective teachers of low SES students we observed is not easily defined. However, these teachers clearly perform functions that quitters and burnouts don't perform, and they are articulate about why they do what they do. As Haberman (1995) said, they have a coherent vision. This is precisely why we must communicate well to our staffing specialists, colleagues, mentors, and university contacts the vision and commitment we want our teachers to possess. When they come across a candidate of excellence, you want your school's name to be the one they think of first.

SUMMARY

In today's world, the human, financial, and material resources you need to create and maintain an exemplary education program that fully meets the needs of all students, including low SES students, isn't going to fall into your lap. The more proactive you are in reaching out to the district central-office decision makers and the various potential outside sources of talent and material support, the more successful your school will be. It's up to you to make the contacts, nurture the relationships, and get the good word out about your school, its vision, its programs, its successes, and its needs. If you don't, who will?

7 Managing Change Successfully

W e read somewhere that in a normal population only 10% to 15% of people are what psychologists would call "change embracers" while the remaining 85% to 90% are "change resisters." Whether or not the numbers are precisely accurate, the fact remains that people's general resistance to change makes instituting change in organizations one of the most difficult challenges leaders face. Bringing about meaningful change in public schools can be even more difficult because seemingly every year teachers are required to master and teach the latest and greatest program to improve reading or math or spelling scores, only to find that this year's innovations are inevitably replaced by next year's. While we're not questioning the efficacy of any of the myriad of learning programs schools adopt from year to year, we recognize that the constant change in emphasis, teaching strategies, or learning materials inevitably creates a certain amount of cynicism among teachers. Why should they spend the time and energy adjusting their teaching methods and styles to the new program when next year it will be something else?

Before we discuss any specific strategies for successfully managing change in your school, we think it's important to point out that the strategies and techniques to improve the education opportunities of low SES children we've discussed in previous chapters don't constitute a new program to be added on top of the existing programs in your school. What we're talking about is a total approach to the education enterprise that applies to every action and interaction that takes place in a school to establish a climate and build the relationships that promote a successful learning experience for every student, regardless of socioeconomic or cultural background. While the strategies we discuss here support the successful implementation of any kind of organizational change, we hope you'll keep the overriding goal of creating a positive learning environment in mind as you think about them.

WHY PEOPLE RESIST CHANGE

Organizational management specialists have identified the key reasons why people, in general—the "change resisters" among us—resist change. The first is fear of the unknown. Security is a basic human need. All of us who took Psychology 101 know that it's the second level from the bottom of Maslow's (1943) hierarchy of needs. Only our physical safety is more basic to us. Even when we're not entirely happy with our current situation, we learn to "live with it" and are wary about what might replace it. Second, change is stressful, even when the result will be a better happier situation. Think about the stress associated with weddings, having a new baby, moving into a new house, or getting promoted to a new and higher position. As leaders and change managers, we can't afford to forget these common human reactions.

In an organizational setting, people tend to fear or resist a change because they worry that the proposed change will

- require them to learn new skills, develop new relationships, or devise new ways to manage their environment that may be less successful than the ones they're used to;
- result in the loss of something they value, for example, power or influence, space, autonomy, or time; or
- produce a level of benefits that may not be worth the effort they'll have to expend to create them.

School faculties and staffs are made up of specialists who operate within fairly narrow parameters. Whether we're talking about teachers in their classrooms, counselors in their offices, administrative assistants in the main office, nurses in their clinics, food service workers in their kitchens and cafeterias, or custodians in their shops, all can, and frequently do, become protective of their "turf." Each has developed his or her own highly developed systems, procedures, and support networks. Because changes anywhere in the school may threaten to upset their systems and networks, they're apt to perceive that their own personal security and success are closely linked with the status quo. Remember the administrative assistants' reaction to the suggestion that the counter that had always separated (protected?) them from visitors in the office be removed? What about the school librarian who routinely uses the hour after lunch to review publishers' catalogs and will now have to supervise the students whom you've excused from music class because of religious sensitivity? And what about the traveling music teacher, who likes to use the same music selections for the concerts in all three schools she serves, when you tell her that the music programs at your school will now include songs suggested by PTA members to showcase the different cultures represented by the students? You'll need to anticipate their possible resistance to the changes you propose to implement and overcome it.

STRATEGIES TO REDUCE RESISTANCE TO CHANGE AND PROMOTE SUCCESSFUL IMPLEMENTATIONS

Many books have been written on the subject of change management, and while the buzz words often change, the four basic strategies for managing change are planning, communication, participation, and leadership. We contend that the modifiers "your" and "proactive" must be added to each.

Planning

Before you undertake any change in your school, you need to develop a comprehensive plan, your road map to the future you envision. If you don't know where you're going, how will you know which road to take or recognize your destination when you get there?

Articulating Your Vision

The first step in your plan is a clear statement of your vision for your school. While a vision or goal statement is a difficult paragraph to write, the process of writing it is critical to the development of the rest of your plan. As you develop your vision statement, consider the following:

- Tie your vision directly to the discontent you want your faculty and staff to experience. Unless the vision is connected to something people want changed, it won't resonate with and motivate your faculty and staff.
- Focus your vision where it matters most. Make it specific and concrete. Word it in a way that makes it tangible for people. Eyes glaze over and cynicism materializes when people hear clichés.
- Make your vision inspirational. The best vision statements lift people up and offer something unexpected, even when it's something people may initially believe is unachievable.
- Think about a demand for change and a vision of a better future as two sides of the same coin. Demand pushes people to want to find a better way, while vision pulls them toward a better future. This push-pull dynamic is the engine that fuels change. Revving up that engine is your job as a leader who seeks to make things better. The secret is to link these two forces closely together.

Developing the Master Plan

Once you have your vision of the future in clear focus in your mind, you'll have the information you need to develop the actual plan. In your plan, you need to identify the following:

- *Parts that make up the whole.* For example, we've talked in this book about the overall school climate, specific teaching strategies and techniques, and strong working relationships with parents, the central office, and the local business community as essential elements in creating and maintaining an education program that provides equal education opportunities for low SES students. The specific elements you need to include in your plan depend, of course, on your particular situation. If you already have a viable student assessment program in place, you don't need to institute a new one. If you already have strong parent participation across your population, you don't need to implement major changes in what you're already doing in this area. Your plan should *acknowledge* what is in place and then focus on the specific areas that could be improved.

- *Logical progression of implementation.* Depending on the scope and depth of the changes you envision, your plan should set clear priorities and divide the effort into workable phases. It should set reasonable (achievable) timelines and include milestones that everyone will be able to recognize as measures of success. While unforeseen circumstances may alter your timelines down the road, it's important for you to set the target you and your faculty and staff are aiming at.

- *Leadership assignments.* While no one can (or ever should) replace you as the overall leader of the change process, you'll certainly need some "deputies" to manage specific activities, and you'll need to line them up as a part of the planning process. You'll need these people "on board at take off" so there's no question in anyone's mind about who's responsible for what. In choosing your leaders, you will, of course, look at the particular strengths they can bring to the change process. While the tendency is to select the natural leaders on your faculty, don't overlook those who tend to be the most change resistant. Enlisting potential naysayers into leadership responsibility can help you get them to buy into the process from the beginning. Recognizing that being selected for leadership responsibility is both a reward and a punishment (extra work), you should talk to your candidates early in your planning and ensure they'll be willing allies in the process.

- *Resources that will be needed.* In your initial planning process, you need to identify the additional resources you may need to implement your plan and line them up in advance. Nothing will frustrate successful implementation of a desired change as quickly as unanticipated obstacles to planned activities. We can't predict what you'll need, but you must. Will you need additional overtime pay resources for custodians who'll have be on duty for additional evening meetings? Will you need additional planning time for faculty meetings or staff development, and will that entail substitute teachers? Will you need access to community centers or local churches for parent meetings? Will you need central office approval for one or more activities? Whatever you think you'll need, you have to make the calls and get at least general approvals before you begin to implement the change process.

- *Language and symbols you'll use to label the future you envision.* Effective change management is future oriented, and the language you use to discuss the future has to be different from the language you use to discuss the present and the past. Give your vision a name, and coin labels for the elements that comprise it. Don't give your faculty and staff any opportunity to think or say, "Been there, done that." If you need help, brainstorm with the leaders you've recruited to facilitate the change process. This will increase their ownership of the change you're instituting and help you identify the words that will resonate with your school community.

Communication

The more people know about what you expect, the more likely they'll be able to meet your expectations. Early, frequent, and continuous communication with the affected faculty and staff will go a long way to ensure the successful implementation of the changes you envision. Once you have your plan in place and your leadership assignments made, you should clearly communicate the following to your entire faculty and staff:

- *Rationale* for the plan you intend to implement, including clear statements of (1) the problem you perceive, (2) the options you've considered for addressing the problem, and (3) the plan you've selected.
- *Process* that will be undertaken.
- *Timeline* and milestones for the process.
- *Leadership assignments* you've made.
- *Benefits you anticipate for the students.* We wholeheartedly believe that the students' welfare is the bottom line for all of your school personnel.
- *Benefits you anticipate for the faculty and staff.* "WIIFM—what's in it for me"—is a top priority for everyone. The more specific you can be here, the better.
- *Benefits you anticipate for your community*—parents, business, other community agencies, and so on.

We strongly recommend that this initial communication be made in a faculty and staff meeting and accompanied by handout materials your faculty and staff can take away to read immediately and refer to over time. In both your oral and written presentations, be sure to use the language and symbols you've identified to label your common future. You need to preclude any comparisons with the present or past.

During the change process, you'll need to continue to communicate regularly with everyone on your faculty and staff. Report progress and celebrate breakthroughs. Don't let anyone think that the process is doing anything except moving forward on schedule. If snags develop, communicate those as well, along with the actions being taken to mitigate the problems and assurances that the process is still on target. Once the process begins, you and your faculty and staff are a team and need to continue to think and act like one. You want to be sure you leave no room for speculation or grapevine gossip that could undermine your efforts.

In addition to communicating effectively inside your school, it's equally important that you communicate similarly with your patrons and the district's central office. As we discussed in Chapter 4, the more you communicate with the parents of your students, the more supportive they can and will be of what you're doing. Similarly, the more your central office superiors know about what you're doing and why, the more supportive they can be of your efforts. And if you do your job well, they'll all learn to speak the same language regarding, and voice approval of, the improvements you're making. Don't forget that they can learn from you.

Participation

For the changes you envision to be successfully implemented, *all* affected faculty and staff have to feel part of the process. This is, of course, where it gets tricky. The overall plan has to be yours, but that doesn't mean that you can't involve your faculty and staff in many of the details of its implementation. As we mentioned in Chapter 3, discovery learning is a powerful learning tool. Just as Socrates guided his students to conclusions he'd already reached, you can enlist your faculty and staff to come up with important details of your plan. To the extent that they see the future as you do, they'll become stronger advocates for the actions you've already identified as necessary. They'll be able to take ownership of your vision.

Throughout the change process, you need to actively work with your faculty and staff and listen to them. They may be able to identify potential obstacles to your plan. If so, you need to acknowledge them and address them. You also need to pay attention to the strongest change resisters and enlist their efforts to overcome whatever problems they foresee.

Bureaucratic cultures (yes, schools are bureaucratic cultures) are often hostile to aspirations. They tend to encourage pragmatism, practicality, and incremental approaches. So expect good faculty and staff members to "protect" you by urging you to lower your aspirations and do only what other schools are doing.

You may be tempted to try to get everyone on board at the same time, but don't. Accept that some important people or groups are going to be opposed to the changes you want to make. Listen to them, *manage* their resistance, but *don't* appease them by watering down the impact of the changes you want to make. Instead, focus your attention and theirs relentlessly on meeting the needs of the students and community you're there to serve.

It's also important to recognize that people often need time to experience a change before they can embrace it. Remember that it probably took you months to come up with your plan, and your faculty and staff are that many months behind you in their thinking. This means you have to allow time for them to catch up to where you are. Be patient and sincere in answering their questions, addressing their concerns, and reiterating your convictions.

Leadership

Leadership is all about winning followers. We have found that simply articulating a demand for change won't work unless you can (1) put your faculty and staff in touch with *why* they should be discontent with the status quo and (2) provide a compelling vision of a better future for them and the school community they serve. These two forces, when melded together, become an engine that can create enough power to overcome apathy.

Your commitment as the executive of the changes you propose must be clear and personal, rather than directed. Regardless of the leadership responsibilities you've assigned, you must be seen as the committed leader of the process. You can't simply delegate overall leadership to others while you handle other critical affairs of the school. Your faculty and staff need to see you actively involved every day in the effort and fulfilling your role in it.

In addition to developing and publishing your vision statement and action plan, identifying the people in charge of the various elements of the plan and providing the necessary resources, you also need to support the process. This means that you need to build stability into a changing environment. It's important to recognize that change is disruptive in itself. You must be available to listen to concerns of faculty and staff, and you must be responsive to those concerns. You have to make sure that the change process doesn't interfere with the day-to-day activities of your faculty and staff, and you should accommodate or mitigate any time-management issues that may arise.

You also need to understand that people need time to disengage from the present before they can embrace the future. Some of your teachers will be slower to implement the strategies and techniques prescribed by the plan. The old saying that "Rome wasn't built in a day" applies to the work you're doing. Praise and reward successful efforts by your faculty and staff and don't punish efforts that fail to meet your standards. Instead, support and counsel your faculty and staff in all their efforts.

SUMMARY

Machiavelli (1952) said, "It must be considered that there is nothing more difficult to carry out, nor more doubtful of success, nor more dangerous to handle, than to initiate a new order of things" (p. 49). We agree and disagree. Bringing about change is a matter of thoughtful and comprehensive planning, carefully crafted communication, significant involvement of all participants, and effective leadership. If you take the time and effort to do it right, we believe you'll succeed in the achieving the ends you seek.

8 Selecting the Right People

In a perfect world, principals would be able to hand pick their faculties and staffs. That, however, is rarely the case. In our experience, even when principals can interview and recommend candidates, teacher and staff assignments are most often made by the district's central human resources department. And, unfortunately, specific placements may depend on lots of things that have little to do with matching teachers' and staffs' qualifications, aptitudes, and interests with particular schools' specific and unique needs. In many districts, union contracts require placements made on the basis of seniority. Other placements may be based on the need to find "new homes" for teachers and others who are being displaced by school downsizing or school closings. Frequently, human resources departments approve transfers requested by employees to buildings that are closer to their home neighborhoods to mitigate some hardship. While we expect that as principal you have the opportunity to interview the candidates before the assignments are finalized, the bottom line is that your choices are often very limited. How then can you leverage the limited authority you have to maximize your ability to staff your school with the right people? In this chapter, we discuss elements of the staff selection and placement process over which you have the most control.

Right up front we need to point out that your not being able to hand pick your staff from the ground up is probably not a completely bad thing. It's human nature that we're most comfortable in the presence of people who are most like us. Given the freedom to do so, we would likely surround ourselves with people who share our values and attitudes, background, experience, language, and culture—creating a faculty and staff of like-minded clones. Given the multicultural nature of our society, and the fact that there's a wide variance in the communities we serve, it's to our advantage to have as diverse a faculty and staff as possible.

That said, what can you do to build a faculty and staff that will be willing and able to create the learning environment you envision—the education program that will provide equal opportunities for all of your students? In our minds there are five areas over which you have considerable control:

1. Identifying the characteristics and qualifications you're looking for
2. Assessing your faculty and staff's strengths and weaknesses to clarify your needs
3. Communicating your needs and interests to central office human resources
4. Structuring the interview process
5. Managing the interview and selection process

IDENTIFYING THE CHARACTERISTICS AND QUALIFICATIONS YOU'RE LOOKING FOR

Before you go shopping for groceries, clothes, lawn mowers, home entertainment equipment, automobile insurance, or an Internet service provider, you make at least a mental list of what you're shopping for. What, exactly, do you want or need? The same is true when you're shopping for faculty or staff. Your first task is to identify, as specifically as possible, the characteristics and qualifications you need in the person who will fill a vacancy on your faculty or staff. And, we recommend that you write this particular list down and keep it at hand for future reference.

In creating your list of qualifications, you need to think about the demographics of your school population, your education program, and your school climate. Do you need leaders or loyal followers; do you need specific multilingual abilities; do you need warm "mothering" skills or strong male role models; do you need especially strong math or reading expertise; do you need teachers who work well on teams or those who can work effectively on their own? We offer these suggestions only as starting points for your thinking. Two of us remember interviewing, decades ago, teachers to staff a new model middle school and looking for what we called "the sparkle factor," meaning a kind of charisma that would appeal to and grab the attention of our seventh and eighth graders most effectively and promote the innovative education program we'd designed.

Whatever list of qualifications you come up with, they're in addition to the basic education and experience requirements for personnel in your district that register first with the human resources department. We can't tell you what those qualifications are, but you have to be able to articulate them. You wouldn't go shopping for a cell phone provider without thinking seriously about your needs. Why would you not practice the same due diligence when shopping for faculty and staff?

ASSESSING YOUR FACULTY AND STAFF'S STRENGTHS AND WEAKNESSES TO CLARIFY YOUR NEEDS

Closely tied to identifying the qualifications and characteristics you're looking for in selecting your faculty and staff is an honest assessment of where you are at the moment. Having thought about what your ideal faculty and staff would look like, you need to evaluate what you already have in place. In the world of business, this comes under the heading of *succession planning*. If you managed a professional sports franchise, it would be the planning you do before the draft or the final trade deadline. In both cases, it has both near and long-term implications. Suppose Marion Brown, one of your first-grade teachers, has announced she's retiring in June, after 20 years at your school. You'll need to replace her with another first-grade teacher. The question is, do you need another Marion Brown, or do you need a first-grade teacher who can also be a strong male role model and speak a second language, preferably Spanish? Or imagine that one of your sixth-grade teachers is halfway through her master's program and is planning to apply for a principalship when she's completed it. Her potential departure is a year or so down the road, but if or when she does go, what will you be looking for in her replacement?

You can't answer either of these questions effectively unless and until you've assessed the staff you currently have. This assessment is not the same as routine teacher or staff evaluations. It's a matter of matching the characteristics your ideal staff would have with what's in place. Make a list of the characteristics and qualities your ideal staff would possess. Score your current faculty and staff on the basis of this list. Identify the areas of weakness and make a wish list so you can focus your attention on them when you have the opportunity to fill a vacancy. If you know what you're looking for, you're more apt to find it.

COMMUNICATING YOUR NEEDS AND INTERESTS TO HUMAN RESOURCES

In Chapter 6, we discussed the value and necessity of developing and maintaining a strong working partnership with the district's central office personnel. Since, in most cases, these are the people with the final authority to hire and place faculty and staff in your building, you need to make sure that you and they are on the same team. When it comes to staffing issues, you need to remember that the people in the human resources department are focused on the district as a whole, while your attention is focused exclusively on your own building. Depending on the size of your school district, that can mean a significant disparity in perspectives. The human resources staff is, of course, concerned about verifying appropriate qualifications and certifications, but beyond that, staffing issues are basically a matter of numbers. Class sizes and the resulting staffing allowances take priority, in their minds, over matching individuals to the most educationally desirable location. You, on the other hand, don't just want a warm body to fill a place on your faculty or staff; you want the *right* person in every position.

How do you overcome the general differences in perspectives and enlist the cooperation of the human resources staff in getting the right people on your faculty and staff? First, do your homework and make sure you know what you're looking for in a replacement for, or addition to, your faculty or staff. Then when you notify human resources about an upcoming vacancy, spell out exactly what qualifications and characteristics you're looking for in the candidates. Ask them to review the resumes of potential candidates looking for the particular combination of knowledge, skills, and experience you seek and select those to be interviewed based on that review. If possible, ask to see the resumes of all potential candidates, and work with human resources to narrow the search to the most promising candidates before you start the formal interview process. Without the specifics you provide, all of the candidates who have the basic qualifications look alike to human resources.

In addition to being specific about your needs and interests when a vacancy occurs on your faculty or staff, you should also be talking to the human resources department on a regular basis about your overall long-term interests in staffing your school. Based on the wish list you developed when you assessed your current staff, talk to human resources at every opportunity about the programs you're implementing and the specific staffing needs you'd like to address. Plant seeds whenever you can and water them with regular reminders. Unless you tell human resources what you need, there's no way they'll be able to provide it.

STRUCTURING THE INTERVIEW PROCESS

When you have the opportunity to interview candidates for a vacancy in your building, take full advantage of it. Read, or reread, the resumes of all the candidates carefully before you interview anyone. Don't be afraid to pick up the telephone and seek additional information about prospective candidates, and don't put too much trust in all the reference letters that accompany the resumes. You're about to choose someone to join your school community, someone you'll be working with and in whose hands you'll be placing the education of your students, someone for whom you'll be held accountable by your teachers, your students, and your students' parents. The more you know about your candidates, the better prepared you'll be to talk with them. Based on what the resumes do and don't tell you, plan your interviews by identifying the specific information you want to gather, and write down the questions you'll ask. Frame the questions in ways that will elicit responses that include explanations and descriptions from your candidates and reveal their attitudes and values rather than just concise statements of fact. Ask the same questions of all candidates so that you have comparable information about each of their potentials to succeed in your school when you've finished.

Begin each interview with a well-thought-out, but brief, description of your school, its demographics, its educational programs, and your primary goals so the candidates can readily relate their experiences to your school setting. Be sure to mention one or two programs about which you're most excited so you can gauge the degree to which each candidate might be supportive of the programs and what each might contribute to them. Tell each candidate about the interview process you're using, including the fact you'll be taking some notes about their responses for future reference. When you've asked your questions and have listened carefully to the responses, invite the candidates to tell you anything else they would like you to know about them, and to ask you any questions they have about your school. The goal of the interview process is to share enough information between you and the candidate so that you both can form a strong impression of whether or not there might be a good match.

At the end of the formal interview, take each candidate on a short tour of the building and introduce him or her to everyone on your faculty and staff you meet. Observe how the candidates relate to the environment, what gets their attention, and how they interact with others. Listen attentively to what they say about your school. Conclude your interview with information about the selection process, who will contact them, and when you expect a decision to be made. When each interview is over, review and clarify your notes while the information and your impressions are still fresh in your mind.

MANAGING THE INTERVIEW AND SELECTION PROCESS

Unless you've been named principal of a school that's still being built and authorized to select your entire faculty and staff, you don't get all that many chances to select your own people. Every vacancy you have is, therefore, an important opportunity for you to move your education program forward, and you don't want to squander it. We've talked about the necessary preparation; now let's talk about follow-through.

The faculty or staff member you want is one who can and wants to contribute to the education program of your school. The interview is, essentially, your first and last chance to both accurately assess each candidate's potential for success in your particular school and sell your school to the candidate you want. Both you and the candidates have a decision to make. To us, there are a number of considerations to ensure the effectiveness of this two-sided process.

Put Your Best Foot Forward

While the candidates you're interviewing want to make a good impression on you, you also need to make a good impression on them—all of them, because you don't know in advance which one you'll prefer. Your office should be neat and well organized and demonstrate that you run a well-managed school. Your office staff should know the names of the candidates you're expecting and be prepared to greet them warmly. Once the interview begins, you should not be interrupted by anything except a genuine crisis. Your telephone shouldn't ring; no one should pop his or her head in your door. Your attention should be totally directed to the candidate you're interviewing. Anything else is not only rude but may also suggest a lack of management skills on your part.

Some of you may find asking interview questions awkward and prefer to talk about the education programs of which you're so proud. The more you talk, the less information you get from the person you're interviewing. While you need to provide the candidate with important information about your school, make sure that you give the candidate plenty of time to respond to your questions and provide you with the information you need.

Finally, keep the conversation completely professional. By this we mean that you should never engage in exchanging gossip, express negative thoughts about any of your faculty and staff or those in other buildings, use bad language, share off-color jokes, or permit your candidates to. This may seem unnecessary, but nervousness makes even good people do peculiar things.

Play by the Rules

Workplace discrimination is a deep, dark hole into which many unsuspecting and otherwise well-intentioned people can fall. Title VII of the Civil Rights Act of 1964 and amendments prohibits discrimination in employment on the basis of race, gender, age, national origin, religion, sexual preference, and so on. According to Dunklee and Shoop (2006),

Employment decisions must be based on nondiscriminatory factors. It is important to remember that equal opportunity laws apply to both employees and job applicants and all selection criteria and employ-ment decisions must be based on job-related standards. In other words, any criteria used, information required or interview questions asked must be directly related to required job performance or be jus-tified as a BFOQ [bona fide occupational qualification] for a parti-cular job. (p. 79)

Any question you ask in an interview must, by law, address a BFOQ and/or the job description for the position you're filling. And whatever questions you ask in an interview you must ask of all candidates. You can't adjust the ques-tions you ask based on any differences you perceive in their names, addresses, physical characteristics, and so on. To fill a position in a multicultural school, you can certainly ask all of the candidates whether or not they are fluent in a second language, but you can't ask an Asian-appearing candidate whether or not English is her first language. You can't ask a young woman whether or not she has children at home or intends to start a family soon.

Taking this a step further, even though your wish list might include adding more male teachers to your faculty, gender is *never* a BFOQ, and you can't limit your interviews and employment consideration to male can-didates only. While you may wish for more Spanish-speaking teachers in your building, you can't limit your interviews or overall selection process to candidates who speak Spanish, unless the position you're filling is that of a Spanish language teacher.

Throughout the interview and selection process, it's up to you to ensure that the process is fair and in full compliance with antidiscrimination laws. Limit all of your questions and discussions to issues that are directly related to the school, its programs, and the particular requirements of the position you're filling.

Need a Second Opinion?

Sometimes you may need to be sure that the candidates you're interview-ing will fit with the other members of a team. If this is your situation, it's fine to include members of that team in the interview process. We suggest that as team members who might provide you with the best input, consider using a parent, a staff member, and one or two teachers. And, if you decide to use an interview team, prepare the other members of the team as you have prepared yourself. Have them read the candidates' resumes and discuss the interview questions you've developed with them. Clarify with them what their role in the interviews will be and the information about the candidate on which it's most important for them to focus. And finally, make sure they know, before the process begins, the relative weight their opinions will have on the final decision. Will it be straight majority rule, or will you make the final decision after considering, and perhaps discounting, their opinions? The successful placement of the selected candidate will depend on the degree to which the interview team accepts the final decision.

Don't Let a Good Candidate Get Away

The right person for the vacancy you have is a valuable commodity. You can't afford to let him or her get away from you because of the bureaucracy or timing or anything else. We recommend that you report back to the human resources office immediately following each interview. If you think you've found the right candidate during the first interview, you need to notify human resources so they don't let another principal, who's also interviewing, get there first. Get them to put a "hold," if at all possible, on the candidate you like, pending completion of your scheduled interviews. At the same time, if you just interviewed a nonstarter, from your point of view, you should also notify human resources—not only to reinforce the qualities you're looking for in candidates but also to allow the candidate to interview elsewhere.

Recognize that the candidate you prefer may be being courted by other like-minded principals. With district human resources' advance approval, contact your preferred candidate with a follow-up phone call. Tell him or her how much you enjoyed the interview and how impressed you were with his or her credentials. Qualify your interest, if appropriate, with the disclaimer that you still have other interviews scheduled, and the district can't make a decision until a specified date. Let that person know you're thinking of them, and then send him or her a packet of additional information about your school that will keep him or her thinking about you and your school.

Recruit Talent

The most proactive approach to selecting faculty and staff for your school is recruiting talent from within the system. We don't mean stealing talent from other schools. What we mean is using all of the opportunities you have to learn about teachers and other staff members who might fit particularly well in your school. Someone another principal may be complaining about at your monthly principals' meetings might have the very qualities you'd like to add to your faculty or staff. As a rather extreme example, suppose your colleague in a predominantly middle-class school complains about the attendance secretary he's been assigned. Suppose he says that the woman's English is so heavily accented by Spanish that his patrons find her hard to understand. She might be the perfect person for your attendance secretary position because her first language is Spanish, and 50% of your students are Hispanic. As another example, suppose a colleague complains that one of his first-grade teachers insists on individualizing instruction to the point that the principal never knows where the class will be with the curriculum at the end of the school year. This could be music to your ears. This teacher might be just the person you need to inspire your other primary teachers to individualize instruction and facilitate learning for low SES students who might otherwise struggle.

When you hear about teachers or staff members in other buildings who might be good matches for your school, visit first with their current principals about your interest and seek permission to talk to them directly. Be sure to keep the human resources department in the loop about what you're doing. If you get permission from the current principals, and the prospective staff members show any interest, invite them to meet with you; show them around your school, and provide them with additional information about your school and its programs to read and think about at home. And when you have vacancies on your faculty and staff, contact them and suggest they apply for a transfer to your building; you'll be delighted to interview them.

SUMMARY

You have limited opportunities to build the faculty and staff you need to deliver the education program you envision. When the opportunity arises, you need to give it your full attention and be prepared to succeed. From groundwork with the human resources department to the actual selection process, you need to be proactive in your approach and diligent in your efforts. After all, who'll be held accountable for the success or failure of your school?

Identifying the Core and Individual Competencies That Promote the Most Successful Learning Environment

WHAT WE MEAN BY COMPETENCIES

Although they are not new concepts, the terms *individual* and *organizational* or *core competencies* have become terms of art in the business world in recent years to describe what Kennedy and Dresser (2003) call "the distinguishing and sustaining characteristics of a successful enterprise" (p. 20). Decades ago, McClelland (1973) published research he'd done that showed that employment tests focused only on aptitude and knowledge weren't valid predictors of future job success. He found, instead, that a combination of types and levels of competencies composed of traits, motives, self-image, skills, and knowledge are more likely to produce superior job performance.

McClelland was only the first of many researchers to study the role of competencies in job success. It's only been in recent years, however, that the power of the idea—that individual and organizational competencies can both explain and help improve global competitive advantage—has taken firm hold in the business world. While to our knowledge the concept of a competency-based workplace hasn't found a formal place the field of public education, we think it holds real promise for the education enterprise, especially, in our minds, when the goal is reforming, improving, or refocusing the education program to successfully educate low SES children.

Individual Competencies

If you ask people what they mean by competencies that promote job success, you'll get a wide variety of answers. Some people believe competencies are synonymous with the basic knowledge, skills, and abilities required to effectively perform the functions of a job. Others recognize that, even when a number of people performing the same job have comparable knowledge, skills, and abilities, some of them are just clearly more effective and successful at the job. To explain this, they suggest that these people possess different, less-tangible qualities that explain their observable superior performance. There are stars and there are superstars, and while we can all recognize the differences between them, we are often hard pressed to explain the differences.

Kennedy and Dresser (2003) suggest a metaphor of an iceberg that we find helpful in explaining the concept of competencies. If you picture an iceberg in your mind, the portion of the iceberg that's above the waterline represents the *knowledge* that can be usefully applied to the job and the *skills* demonstrated in the performance of the job. These "above-the-waterline" elements can be strengthened by training and development and are reasonably easy to change. The portion of the iceberg that's below the waterline represents elements or characteristics that are more difficult to change and less responsive to training and development. These elements are more inherent qualities that include, for example, *self-image* (attitudes, values, and identity), *traits* (general dispositions to behave in a certain way), and *motives* (thoughts and impulses to behave in a certain way).

Another way to illustrate what we mean by individual competencies that promote job success is the example of Olympic swimmer Michael Phelps, who in the 2008 summer games won a record eight gold medals. Sports analysts suggested that his incredible success was based on his unique physical gifts and the superior swimsuits he wore. His coach, however, credited Phelps' work ethic, his willingness and ability to practice longer and harder than his competitors, and his ability to focus his mind on the challenge of the moment. Phelps, himself, said simply, "I just hate to lose." We would suggest that Phelps' skills and abilities to swim the four different strokes needed to compete successfully in eight different Olympic events were the result of his "above-the-waterline" training and development. His work ethic, his ability to screen out distractions and focus solely on his own swimming, and his refusal to accept defeat, however, represent "below-the-waterline" characteristics that are inherent in his nature.

How, you ask, does this discussion of competencies relate to developing schools that successfully educate low SES children? To us, the answer is two obvious ways. First, we suggest that not all teachers who have the requisite above-the-waterline knowledge skills and abilities will have the same inherent below-the-waterline competencies that promote successful teaching of low SES children. Similarly, not all school staff members, who have the knowledge, skills, and abilities to perform the functions of their jobs, possess the inherent characteristics that enable some to relate more effectively and successfully with low SES children and their parents. Second, we suggest that, if there are inherent competencies that enable some teachers and staff members to succeed where others might fail, we ought to know what those competencies are so that we can recruit teachers and other staff who possess them.

We also believe there is a third way that thinking in terms of competencies, as we've described them, is relevant to building an education program that ensures equal-education opportunities for all students. If you were one of Phelps' Olympic competitors and heard that the reason he edged you out at the finish by one one-hundredth of a second was his ability to focus and refusal to lose, wouldn't you work hard to develop the same traits in yourself? Knowing that your own physique doesn't match his, wouldn't you train extra hard to get your body in as close to the same shape as possible? We're absolutely convinced that school personnel, faculty, and staff alike, like competitive athletes, want to be as effective as possible in the results of their work. They've obtained the requisite knowledge. They've honed their skills. If others are successful in ways they're not, they want to know the secret of success so they can do the same. It's the under-the-waterline elements that they don't yet understand. Later in this chapter, we'll discuss ways to identify the competencies that promote teaching success with low SES students, but before we do, we need to discuss the concept of organizational competencies.

Organizational or Core Competencies

Hiring or developing staff with critical individual competencies can only promote the success of the overall enterprise if those competencies are relevant to the core mission of the enterprise itself. In the business world, it's the challenges of increasing global competition that encourage corporations to seek ways to focus their financial and human resources on producing the specific products or services that will earn them the largest market share and maximize profits. Companies that, in less competitive markets, dabbled successfully in a variety of undertakings have found that their markets are being taken over by smaller, more-focused companies that produce only one product or service and do so with spectacular results. Their response has been to identify the core competency they possess that sets them apart from their competitors and focus all of their resources and energy toward capitalizing on that market advantage.

Kennedy and Dresser (2008) illustrate what we mean by core competencies in Table 9.1. We think you'll agree with their examples. Each of the companies in Table 9.1 and many other major corporations have found it to their advantage to identify the core competency or "intangible commodity" they're selling that sets them apart from their competitors. We're sure that you can identify the core competencies of many of them based on the logos and words they use to present themselves to the public and the consistently reliable quality of their products or services.

Table 9.1 Strategic (Core) Competencies: Areas for Companies to Achieve Competitive Advantage

Sources of Competitive Advantage	Related Strategic (Core) Competencies
Technology	Communications (Nokia) High-speed processing (Intel) Search (Google)
Quality	Consistency (McDonald's) Engineering (Toyota)
Service	On-time delivery (FedEx) World-class service (Ritz Carlton) Financial risk management (Goldman Sachs)
People/Culture	Fun (Southwest Air) Magic (Disney)

Source: Adapted from Schultze, Bremen, Crandall, & Wallace (1994, p. 6).

Why do we mention corporate core competencies here? We do because we understand that not only are companies able to successfully market their products and services to us through carefully imaged advertising but also because they have a clear focus for selecting, training, and motivating their employees to deliver the promised and expected goods and services—and they deliver! When you go to a McDonald's, you know exactly what you'll get to eat. When you need to send an overnight package that absolutely has to arrive the next morning, your first thought is FedEx. When you buy a new computer, one of the first things you look for is an Intel processor. Why can't the same mind-set work to the advantage of public schools? We think it can.

IDENTIFYING CORE SCHOOL AND INDIVIDUAL COMPETENCIES THAT PROMOTE STUDENT SUCCESS

As a principal, you have a clear vision of what your school should look and feel like, how classrooms should operate, and how your students can succeed. You also know what you're looking for when you hire a new teacher or counsel a struggling one. The key to making your vision a reality is getting everyone on your staff not only to recognize it but also to strive for it and achieve it. In our experience, every faculty and staff has its few natural superstars (your Michael Phelpses), its couple of "duds," and all the others in between, who are willing and able and could be great, if only you knew how to show them the way to greatness. Like Socrates, we don't think the answer is "out there somewhere"; we believe it's already in the minds of you and your faculty and staff waiting to be drawn out, verbalized, internalized, and put into action.

Identifying Your School's Core Competency

As it is for corporations in a highly competitive economy, the starting point for mobilizing your resources to successfully achieve your vision, we contend, is to clearly identify your school's core competency. As we noted earlier, you don't get to select your entire faculty and staff; you mostly inherit them. And most of your faculty and staff think that their jobs are to teach the third-grade curriculum, or to manage the attendance records, or to keep the building systems operating and the sidewalks shoveled, or to provide educational services to students for whom English is a second language. They see their jobs, first and foremost, as fulfilling their job descriptions and focus their efforts inside fairly narrow parameters. In other words, they often exhibit tunnel vision. Conversely, Southwest Airlines employees see their jobs, whatever their particular functions, as making air travel fun, and Disney employees see their jobs, whatever their specific functions, as creating a magical experience for their guests. The difference in attitudes is significant and attributable to the existence of a corporate culture built around the core corporate competency. Are you with us? There is incredible power in not only having a vision but in it giving it a name and creating a culture around it.

In the world of big business, identification of the core competency is the responsibility of the top executives in consultation with the board of directors and the senior marketing analysts who set corporate direction. In the school setting, we believe that the core competency of your school can, with your leadership and vision, be identified by your faculty and staff to maximum effectiveness.

Wait! Don't tell us you can't see how a big business organizational and marketing strategy can apply to your school and your students! If you can't see yourself presenting the idea of an "organizational core competency" to your faculty and staff, phrase it a different way. It's not what you call it that matters, but the centrality of the concept. Call it a vision or mission, goal or target, or any other word you can use to make it the focal point of your school's efforts, the marketing tool you use to enlist parents and businesses to your cause, the principle that guides your decision making, and the rallying cry when your faculty's and staff's spirits sag. Whatever you call it, you can only benefit from a core idea that guides everyone's thinking about what you're doing and why. While we're a bit loathe to admit it, President Bush and his political advisors really nailed it with the title *No Child Left Behind* for his landmark legislation package. We all may have problems with the details and the mandates and the consequences of the law and its application, but we find it hard to argue with the *sentiment* in terms of our particular interest in ensuring equal education opportunities for low SES children.

In our experience, the most effective way to identify the core competency of a school is to involve the entire faculty and staff in the process. We believe that, deep down, everyone who works in a public school has made a conscious choice to do so and has made that choice for a reason. For the committed professionals on your faculty, the reason is obvious: They want to educate children, and they have studied long and hard to acquire the skills to do so. For others on your staff, there are other employers of secretaries, nurses, cooks, custodians, and so on who, potentially, pay higher salaries and wages. Whether their immediate motivation is to work close to home or for longer summer vacations, they too have chosen to work in a school and, in some way or another, believe they're making an important contribution to society. Everyone who works in your school should have a personal stake in its success, and this is a valuable tool in your tool bag. Those who don't have such a commitment don't belong in your school, and it should become easier for you to recognize them and "counsel" them out or "trade" them for others whose commitment is authentic and strong.

The process we recommend is a thought process that can't be accomplished in a *single* all-staff meeting. We recommend that you present the initial challenge at an all-staff meeting and carefully explain what a core competency (or whatever name you give it) is and what its value will be to the school, perhaps as we've explained it here. Ask (even better, require) everyone to submit his or her idea for the school's core competency to you in writing within a stated time frame. The question you should ask is, "What is it about our approach to educating children that sets us apart from other schools?" Review the submissions with your leadership team and see if there's a consensus. At a subsequent all-staff meeting, present the results of the exercise. If there was a clear consensus, but various wordings of the same sentiment, use the meeting to get agreement on the two to four words that you can all agree represent your core competency. If there was no consensus evident with the original submissions, present the several concepts that were most frequently suggested and discuss them. If necessary, ask your faculty and staff to think about the alternatives presented at the meeting and submit refinements to you, until you get to a statement of your core competency to which everyone can agree and, most important, personally commit. The final wording is less important in the long run than the process of getting everyone on your staff thinking about what you're doing and why. Off the tops of our heads, how about "Our kids come first," or "We care about everyone," or "We're determined to succeed," or "Teamwork works," or "Whatever it takes," or "We believe we can." Once you've identified the core competency, you can use it to define the culture of your school. As an added benefit, you now have a new marketing tool to solicit both parent and business support for your school.

Identifying the Individual Competencies That Promote Success in Your School

In Chapter 3, we noted that the teachers we observed were identified for us by their principals based on their proven ability to successfully teach low SES students, enabling these children to overcome any deficits in their school-readiness skills and finish the school year at or near grade level. If you remember, the focus of our study was to identify strategies and techniques successful teachers of low SES students use to create a positive learning environment and promote a successful learning experience for these students. In that chapter, we described those strategies and techniques and recommended that you implement them in your own school.

What we didn't discuss in Chapter 3 is that the teachers we observed weren't *directed* to use the strategies and techniques. The strategies and techniques we observed were developed independently by those teachers based on what we see as under-the-waterline qualities or competencies these teachers possess. In their own way, these exemplary teachers are the Michael Phelpses in their schools.

If individual competencies make the difference between good teachers and great ones, we need to be able to recognize them when we see them, name them, and make them visible to everyone. By way of illustration, in Table 9.2, we list the four successful teaching strategies we discussed in Chapter 3 (plus a wild card we call *charisma*) and examples of individual competencies we believe promote success in the results of their implementation.

Table 9.2   Individual Competencies That Support Specific Education Strategies

Strategy	Competencies
Building positive relationships	Ability to inspire trust "Gift of gab" Friendly nature "Customer service" mentality Reliability Responsiveness Openness to different ideas Appreciation of differences Honesty and candor Perseverance
Conducting formative and summative assessments	Attention to detail Organizational skills Powers of observation Facility with technology
Integrating learning experiences	Ability to see the big picture Ability to multitask Imagination Creativity Agile memory Curiosity Open-mindedness
Creating a positive learning environment	Patience Flexibility, adaptability Facility with languages "Salesmanship" Sense of humor Trusting nature Love of and respect for learning
Charisma	Self-confidence Optimism Trustworthiness Leadership Common sense Decisiveness Team player "Sparkle"

Whether you agree or disagree with our take on the individual competencies (under-the-waterline qualities) we identify above, we know you'll strongly agree that there is more than a teaching certificate and regular continuing education credits involved in one's success in the classroom or anywhere else in your school. As we mentioned earlier, you know what you're looking for when you hire teachers or other staff members for your building, and what you're looking for goes beyond the basic credentials required for the job. You know who your superstars are, and, we believe, you'd love to spread their magic around to all of your faculty and staff. We suggest that focusing your faculty and staff's attention on the individual competencies that promote success is an effective way to begin that process.

There are basically two ways to focus your faculty and staff's attention on the individual competencies that promote the optimal learning experience for your students, and especially your low SES students. One is from the bottom up, the other is from the top down, and there are benefits and consequences to both.

The from-the-bottom-up process is a concerted staff development effort conducted over a period of time, perhaps a full school year in length, in which you would ask your faculty and staff to identify the personal qualities they see as most necessary to successfully carrying out your mission—delivering on your core competency. In our experience, this can be a very time-consuming process that involves a steep learning curve before most people can get past thinking about the requisite above-the-waterline skills and abilities and focus on the below-the-waterline personal traits, attitudes, qualities, and so on. The upside of this process is that, by the time the process is complete, everyone will certainly have internalized that key difference and be thinking in terms of the individual competencies they need to develop in their own work. The downside is the time involved and the strong possibility that the effort will have to be shelved in favor of dealing with "here and now" issues, before you "get there."

The top-down process requires you, the principal, to identify in your own mind the individual competencies that set your superstars apart from your other faculty and staff. Having clarified your thinking about what it really takes to create the most effective learning environment and meet the needs of every student in your school, you then need to analyze your faculty and staff and identify the specific competencies your less than fully successful faculty and staff may be lacking. As a result of your ongoing analysis, you can work individually with each person to make him or her aware of the quality that seems to be lacking. *Susan's too impatient; she doesn't give the shy children time to get up their courage to answer her questions. John's a little inflexible in his schedule. He ends a lesson because the clock says it's time to move on, even when there's really good learning taking place. Mary needs to develop a sense of humor; she frequently overreacts to students' antics. Marsha's never rude to parents who come into the office, but she doesn't smile and make them feel welcome.*

SUMMARY

We believe there's real power in understanding the significant impact core competencies and people's individual competencies have on the overall success of your education program. When you involve your faculty and staff in identifying and naming your school's core competency, you focus their attention on the essence of your vision and enable them to develop a common, positive approach to achieving it in which they all now have a vested interest. When you've identified the specific individual competencies you're looking for in your faculty and staff, you can focus your interview and selection process on determining the degree to which candidates already possess them. You can also influence the development of critical competencies among your existing faculty staff by identifying those competencies and making them visible to your faculty and staff and coaching your people about them. When they know what competencies work best and will be rewarded with success, they'll strive to develop them. We discuss ways to manage faculty and staff performance around your specific expectations in the next chapter.

10 Identifying Expectations and Managing Performance

N ow, because you worked your way through the first nine chapters, we have to assume that you have a genuine interest in making whatever changes are needed in your school to enhance equal education opportunities for low SES students—in our minds a difficult, but certainly worthy and courageous, goal. Our objective in this chapter is to support your efforts to successfully implement the changes you want to bring about by reviewing performance management strategies and techniques that will enable you to do just that.

We know that your professional responsibilities as principal include annual or periodic faculty and staff evaluations, conducted in a formally pre-scribed manner. This chapter, on performance management, we emphatically state, has *nothing* to do with your formal evaluation process. Instead, this chapter focuses on aligning your day-to-day leadership and management activities *directly* with your intent to implement changes you need in the school climate, teaching strategies or techniques, parent involvement, and so on. We aren't talking here about layering on another level of management responsibility; rather, we're talking about an approach to leading and manag-ing your faculty and staff that will make your day-to-day efforts more effective, and . . . wait for it . . . easier.

SOME BASIC ASSUMPTIONS

Our discussion of effective performance management strategies and techniques is based on a starting point that comprises six assumptions about people in general, and your faculty and staff in particular. Our assumptions follow:

1. A significant majority of people are naturally resistant to change.

2. People's resistance to change is frequently based on their concerns that the change will
   a. require them to learn new skills, develop new relationships, or devise new ways to manage their environments that may be less successful than the ones they're used to; or
   b. result in the loss of something they value, for example, power or influence, space, autonomy, or time.

3. Employees, in general, want to be as successful in their work as possible, want to meet their bosses' expectations, and believe that they are doing so on a day-to-day basis.

4. Professionals in the field of education (teachers, administrators, counselors, specialists, nurses, etc.) chose this field because they love children, are dedicated to the concept of education, and believe in its value to our society.

5. Each person who works in a public school setting has made a conscious choice to do so and believes he or she is contributing, if even in some small way, to their community. (Those that don't generally can be convinced to find another job that pays more and demands less.)

6. *If* your faculty and staff are *not* meeting your expectations, it's because *they don't know what your expectations are.*

COMMUNICATING YOUR EXPECTATIONS

We anticipate that, while most of you nodded in agreement as you read the first five assumptions above, a number of you may have said, "Whoa!" regarding the sixth. Our 75 or more years of experience in public education, higher education, and the business world support the efficacy of this assumption and its importance to effective leadership and performance management. It's human nature to assume that the people around us think the way we do and share the same understandings. We couldn't be more mistaken in that belief. Want to check that out? Present this scenario to five people with whom you work:

Your 12-year-old son tells you he's going out to play football with his buddies. You say, "You can't go out until you've cleaned your bedroom!" After the usual hassle, your son goes to his room to clean it and soon reports that he's finished and is going out to join his friends. You say, "Just a minute, let me see what you've done."

Now ask your colleagues to make a list of evidence they would look for in determining whether or not the boy's room was clean—what would their expectations be regarding a clean bedroom? We can guarantee that there will be little, if any, agreement between you and your five colleagues regarding those expectations. It's a cautionary tale.

The point here is that you must communicate your expectations in clear, specific terms. Regardless of the discussions you've had at faculty and staff meetings and the general agreement you've heard about the actions you're all going to take, everyone's mental picture of what those actions look like and what results will be achieved are inherently different.

To effectively communicate your expectations you need to

- identify the goal or target;
- specify the actions to be taken;
- identify the behaviors needed to undertake the actions required to reach the goal or target;
- set a time frame in which the goal or target is to be achieved; and
- specify the observable results that will be evident when the goal or target is achieved.

As an example, in Chapter 4, we talked about creating a welcoming climate in the school that would encourage and enable low SES parents to become active participants in the school. Let's call that the goal or target you're expecting your office staff and others to achieve. How would you most effectively communicate your expectations? We'd suggest taking actions like the following:

- Barrier-like counter removed
- TV monitor with computer slide show installed in the main lobby
- Photos of students in and out of school to be added regularly to the slideshow
- Office personnel to greet everyone who enters the office immediately
- Security procedures to be carried out correctly, but in a friendly, nonaggressive manner
- All visitors to be escorted to appropriate room or office and introduced

Behaviors needed to create the welcoming environment might include the following:

- All faculty and staff stop what they're doing and immediately acknowledge visitors to the building
- All visitors are greeted with a smile and a warm greeting
- Office personnel introduce themselves to visitors by first and last name, not a title
- All faculty and staff members who meet a visitor in the hallways greet the visitor, introduce themselves by first and last name, and inquire if the visitor needs any assistance

The time frame in which to achieve the goal might be

- immediately, in the case of expected faculty and staff actions and behaviors; or
- within two weeks, to get the counter removed and the TV installed.

Observable results that will indicate the goal has been achieved:

- Office staff regularly observed stopping their work and acknowledging visitors as soon as they enter the office area, even if it's a "just a minute and I'll be with you" signal
- Office staff regularly observed greeting guests with a smile, a first and last name introduction, and a "How can I help you?"
- Faculty and others regularly observed acknowledging and engaging visitors in the hallways
- Counter removed and TV installed and slideshow running within time frame specified
- Parents visiting the school appear comfortable and relaxed when dealing with school personnel
- No reports of parents refusing or hesitating to make and keep appointments when invited by faculty and staff
- Low SES parent attendance at school events steadily increases within the first nine weeks

Is this level of specificity necessary, you ask? Yes it is! You know what you want, and the only way you're going to get it is to spell it out. Asking your office staff to "be friendlier" isn't going to achieve the goal you have in mind, and their actions won't necessarily match your mental picture of *friendlier*. The same is true if you want your faculty to do a better job of integrating instruction or creating an environment in their classrooms that's "more conducive to learning." The clearer you communicate your expectations, the more likely your faculty and staff will be able to meet them. An important note here: Communicating your expectations and managing performance around them is a future-oriented process. There's no need to look backward at what you've done before, and there's no advantage in even suggesting that there was anything wrong with how people went about their jobs previously. The message you need to convey is that these are the things we're going to focus on going forward. The argument "But, we've never done it this way before" should not be a relevant criticism in your school, and your faculty and staff need to know that.

Communicating Group Expectations

When you're communicating expectations that apply to multiple members of your faculty and staff, it's a good idea initially to share them in group meetings. This not only reduces the amount of time you have to spend talking about your expectations but also ensures that every member of the group gets the same message in the same words. Further, it conveys the idea that each particular group is a team and encourages them to work together to achieve the goals or targets you've set for them.

Depending on the specific makeup of the group and your "history" together, you may find it beneficial to enlist their assistance in identifying the specific actions, behaviors, time frames, and expected results that will support and achieve the goal you've set. If, as a group, they have the requisite knowledge and experience to contribute effectively, then their active participation in setting expectations can only increase their buy-in. Because people can be suspicious and wary of any change, you must entertain their questions and concerns and respond to them thoughtfully and helpfully. This doesn't mean backing off your goal, but rather mitigating their fears and enabling them to move forward.

Communicating Individual Expectations

There will, undoubtedly, be occasions when there are specific individuals who need to make some changes in the way they go about their duties. It might be a first-year teacher who lacks the experience to meet the full expectations that you have for the fully experienced faculty. It might be a new counselor or specialist who hasn't yet developed an understanding of the education program and school climate of your particular building. Or, it might be a veteran teacher who is very set in his or her ways and is finding it difficult to make the adjustments you expect of the others. If you individualize instruction for your students, you can certainly individualize instruction for your faculty and staff.

You should schedule meetings to communicate individual expectations in advance and hold them in private. You should tell the individuals what the meeting is about so their heads will be in the same place as yours when you meet. And your "invitation" to the meeting should never create fear. You might say, for example, "I'd like to talk to you about some ways to individualize your teaching even more than you do now." Or, "I have some thoughts to share with you about ways to get the shyer kids in your class more actively involved."

As we've discussed above, the focus of the meeting is what your expectations are going forward, stated as specifically as possible—what, when, how, and what results will evidence success. It's always a good plan to get your people to feed back to you their understanding of what you're expecting of them and to deal attentively with any questions or concerns they may raise. They need to leave your office with a clear understanding of your expectations and useable advice and counsel about exactly what they can do to meet them.

Setting Reasonable Expectations

One of the great maxims of childrearing and school administration is never threaten a punishment you aren't prepared to deliver. If you do, you risk losing your authority. We believe the converse is equally true: Never set your expectations so high that they can't reasonably be achieved. It's a sure way to lose your faculty and staff's respect and undermine your credibility as a leader.

We have no idea of the scope of the changes you'll need to make to achieve your vision for your school, just as we have no way of appreciating the level of talent you have on your faculty and staff. Only you can know what you want to accomplish and what you have to work with. We strongly recommend, however, that you lay out a master plan, prioritize the specific changes needed, and develop an incremental plan to reach your goals. And this applies both to schoolwide expectations and those you have for individuals on your faculty and staff. Be careful not to set the bar too high or attempt more changes than people can reasonably address at the same time. Think carefully about the timelines you expect to be met. Make sure they are both relevant and realistic. Be willing to adjust your expectations if unexpected pressures or changing events occur. Finally, be prepared to provide your active support in helping individuals and groups achieve the vision. Don't micromanage, of course, but show continuous interest and willingness to support.

MANAGING PERFORMANCE AROUND YOUR EXPECTATIONS

Once you've made your plans and identified and communicated your expectations, managing your faculty and staff's performance to reach your expectations is the easy part. Really! To the extent that you've clearly communicated your expectations, managing performance is a matter of observing your faculty and staff in action and providing constructive feedback to reinforce their successes and correct their missteps.

You already spend the majority of your time observing the operations of your school, listening to reports of successes or problems that have occurred, patting people on the back, or helping them solve problems they're having. Having clearly communicated your expectations, you now have a shared frame of reference around which to structure your day-to-day interactions with staff. You can shape your "good job" conversations as positive feedback directly related to the expectations you've previously identified. For instance, you might say, "So you got Alice to read aloud in class today just by letting her sit on the floor? That certainly shows your classroom feels safe to her. Good job; great breakthrough." You can frame your criticism of a less-than-visitor-friendly office assistant in terms of, "I thought we'd agreed we're going to greet every visitor with a smile as soon as they come in and make them feel welcome. I'm not sure Mrs. Jones felt welcome this morning." Managing performance around your expectations simply means having an ongoing series of nonconfrontational conversations about mutually agreed upon goals.

What If You're Wrong?

To paraphrase Robert Burns's famous quote, the best-laid plans of mice and men often go astray. It's conceivable that even the best-thought-out game plan can include a miscalculation of some sort. If the expectations you have identified prove to be unachievable in some way, you should recognize and acknowledge the fact and revise your expectations. If, in the course of your ongoing conversations with your faculty and staff, you become aware of legitimate frustrations, you'll need to rethink your expectations. If you manage your own expectations and make needed adjustments while still keeping your eye on the goal, you'll only increase your chances for success. By acknowledging your error and communicating your revised expectations, you'll also enhance your position as an education leader with your faculty and staff.

PROVIDING CONSTRUCTIVE FEEDBACK

Although you've undoubtedly heard this before, we think we'd be remiss if we didn't talk about effective ways to provide feedback to your faculty and staff regarding your expectations to maximize the probability of achieving the ends you intend. We all know what kind of feedback we'd like to get regarding our efforts, and when. We want recognition when we've done a good job. We need reinforcement when we're doing well so we know we're on the right track. If we're making a mistake, we want to know about it as soon as possible so we can correct it before it's too late. Unfortunately, it's easy to forget that other people need the same thing we do when we get caught up in the hectic business of the day. So, here's our quick review of the art of giving constructive feedback—praise and criticism.

Praise is the most effective and inexpensive resource available to you in managing your faculty and staff. Giving praise is a simple technique, and when it's done right, it has a ripple effect. Not only does it provide a reward and recognition to the person performing well, but it communicates to the entire faculty and staff that good performance is noticed, appreciated, and will be rewarded. When you use it correctly, praise builds trust between you and your faculty and staff. However, if you bestow praise inconsistently, you confuse and demotivate people.

Criticism can and should be a positive, valuable learning experience for the person being criticized. While it indicates that the recipient has made a mistake or has done something in a way you wish they hadn't, if you deliver it in a way that preserves the person's ego, you enable them to correct the error and move on successfully. That is, after all, what they want to do.

All feedback, both praise and criticism, will be most effective when you deliver it in a timely manner (as close to the event as possible), in an appropriate place, and with enough specificity to be clearly understood. When you catch people doing things right and praise them while their efforts are still fresh in their minds, you underscore the value you place on the specific performances they've delivered. When you criticize a flawed performance as soon as you become aware of it, you give the person the opportunity to correct the behavior before it becomes a bigger problem. You should make sure that all feedback you give is very specifically stated. Save your praise for a private meeting when the praiseworthy performance is unattainable by others or when the praise may cause jealousies or unnecessary animosities. Praise people in public when their performance has been outstanding and maintained over a significant period of time and when their performance represents a solution to a problem of mutual concern to your faculty or staff as a whole. Always deliver corrective comments in private and in person—no notes in mailboxes, e-mails, or voice messages.

Feedback is most effective when it focuses on

- the behavior rather than the person;
- observations rather than inferences;
- descriptions rather than judgments;
- sharing ideas rather than on giving advice; and
- the value to the recipient rather than the person giving the feedback.

Praise is most effective when you

- are consistent in praising good performance whenever you see it;
- are proportionate in the quality of your praise;
- are specific in your praise and focus on the praiseworthy behavior or results, not the recipient; and
- bestow the praise as close to the event as possible.

Criticism is most effective when you

- begin on a positive note before you state the problem;
- criticize an action, behavior, or result and not the person;
- avoid using the word *you;*
- criticize as soon as you notice the behavior and before there's a serious problem;
- ask for feedback from the recipient and listen attentively to his or her responses;
- clearly identify what you want the person to do differently and when;
- provide suggestions regarding how he or she can do it;
- obtain agreement;
- end the conversation on a positive note; and
- look for the earliest opportunity to praise the corrected behavior.

SUMMARY

To get your education program from where it is to where you want it to be, you have to make your goals and the pathway to them visible to your faculty and staff. You need to identify and communicate your expectations for their performance and the results of that performance in the most specific terms possible. To amplify what we said in Chapter 7 regarding change management, if you and your faculty and staff don't know where you're going and by what road, no one will be able to tell how far you are from your goal or when you've achieved it. Managing the performance of your faculty and staff to achieve the vision you have for your school isn't an additional task piled on top of your already busy schedule. Instead, it's a proactive and rational way to manage the day-to-day work of your faculty and staff. It's using your leadership skills to promote the best education program for the children entrusted to you by their parents.

11

A Proven Approach to Improving Educational Opportunities for Low SES Children

In the previous chapters, we've discussed numerous strategies for reshaping and redirecting the professional thinking in schools, particularly in low SES schools. We're not advocating turning your schools upside down with new thinking and new programs as soon as you put this book down. We are saying that the path to change needs to begin *now*. As leaders in your schools, you're the change agents, and contrary to the old saying, this time the buck *starts* with you and ends with your faculty, your students, and their parents. Based on our observations of schools that succeed well in working with low SES students, we see four critical pieces that need to be place for the most effective education to occur. These include

1. professional climate of the school,

2. behavioral climate of the school,

3. community climate, and

4. instructional practices.

And while these areas frequently overlap, there is a clear linear approach to making sure the *whole* includes *all* the parts. The principals we observed shared the goal of building a strong foundation for learning based on these *parts* that will be self-sustaining far beyond their personal tenures in these schools.

PROFESSIONAL CLIMATE

Staff development isn't about programs—it's about attitudes. In every school we observed, the principals believed that the first seed for sustainable change begins in the hearts and minds of the faculty and staff. We tend to forget that everyone in our buildings, teachers and support staff alike, interact daily with students in meaningful ways. One of the principals we observed related that one of her secretaries came to her after the yearbook for that year was published and noted that she was listed on the page for clerical personnel and requested a change for next year's publication. She thought she should be listed on the same page with the teachers. To make her point, the secretary noted that when the children come in with lunch money, she helps them count it. When students need to call home, she helps them memorize their phone numbers and addresses, and when they bring in an excuse, she works with them to write their names clearly. Isn't that teaching? Looking through this new lens, the principal began to reexamine the classifications in her building. She saw that the custodians taught the children how to clean up after themselves, and the food service manager often spoke to the children about being respectful to the cafeteria ladies. The cafeteria ladies spent time everyday helping children count out the right amount of money for lunch, remember to pick up all their food as they walked through the line, and make healthy choices for lunch. Isn't all of that teaching? This principal thought so and expanded, both in her own mind and publicly, the concept that the responsibility for instruction belonged to everyone who interacted with students in the building. She reported that when she put everyone on the same team, it gave the whole faculty and staff a stronger sense of shared purpose and pride in the school's programs.

Once you establish that everyone in the school is an educator in some way, you need to put a process in place to foster collaboration among them. As we all know, the autonomy of the classroom teacher can sometimes be an obstacle to collaboration. However, the teachers we observed had already begun to collaborate with the resource teachers—actually coteaching with them—and that proved to be a valuable key to their success in teaching low SES children.

While this kind of collaboration isn't a program you can mandate in your schools, you can certainly develop a process to create a climate conducive to building the level of trust and shared purpose that promotes collaboration.

One way to do this is to schedule common planning time for the teachers who need to work collaboratively. The principals we observed designed the master schedule to insure that teachers in each grade level met for at least one hour every week. These meetings weren't intended to be social events: They were to be focused on instruction and professional dialogue. To be sure that these meetings wouldn't be used to talk about mundane issues like field trips, school pictures, and recess equipment, the principals established the "rules" for these meetings. In addition to setting professional expectations such as on-time attendance, respectful attention to all ideas, and open sharing of successes as well as disappointments, these rules also required each team to identify at least three long-term goals the team would pursue as grade-level goals. Resource teachers were invited to be part of these meetings and share their strategies for working with children, learn about the curriculum being taught, and offer suggestions about how they could support instruction in the classroom. The teams also shared chapter tests, report cards, standardized test results, and so on, looking for techniques that seemed to work best with students. The principals also required the teams to provide feedback to them following every meeting, so the principal stayed current with the instructional focus and would be able to respond to questions and concerns identified by the teams.

Over time, the meetings resulted in the development of a new level of trust among the teachers as they participated in meaningful discussions of what did and didn't work across the grade level. In addition, the resource teachers began to become part of the classroom instruction and shared their expertise in the classroom along side the teacher, not outside the classroom. As an added bonus, in one of the schools, teachers began to routinely share and provide copies of teaching aids they'd created for their own classrooms with other grade-level teachers.

The principals we observed noted that these collaborative meetings became so internalized as part of the professional climate in their schools that, even if they were to leave or retire, these meetings would be staff driven and continue. It's important to point out that this kind of collaboration doesn't happen overnight. In most cases, it took at least two years to be really embedded in the school culture. It's not a program; it's a process.

As we observed, we saw other techniques principals used to establish a sense of a professional educational community in their schools. While there are too many to mention, we think these will give you some idea of what works.

- Celebration breakfasts before school, or lunches on short days, to celebrate the successes in school. Teachers are encouraged to relate accomplishments by colleagues that may otherwise have gone unnoticed by the total faculty.

- Glad Notes—cheerful cards the principal places in mailboxes when he or she notices good things happening in particular classrooms.
- The 20/20 Club in which every staff member (including teachers, secretaries, custodians, etc.) is asked to mentor a child 20 minutes a week for 20 weeks.
- Occasional food treats the principal places in the staff lounge to say, "Thank you for all you do."
- Creation of a leadership team that, over time, became responsible for school decisions the principal could appropriately delegate.
- Including a degree of collaboration focused on self-reflection and growth as a part of routine teacher evaluations.
- Once a quarter, having grade-level teams visit vertically with the next grade above and below theirs, to understand what instruction looks like at those levels. Teachers were able to learn which skills the higher grade level needs in place to ensure success and also to share those skills they need in place from the lower grades. This provides a flow of instructional responsibility throughout the school year.

All of these small initiatives were started by creative principals with one thought in mind: to build a strong sense of community in the school. One of the principals told us that at the very first staff meeting she attended, a teacher sadly confided that she felt so alone and vulnerable in the school. Later in the school year, this same teacher commented about the positive change in climate and community that had developed. That works for us!

BEHAVIORAL CLIMATE

Teachers can't teach and children can't learn in a school that doesn't feel safe, ordered, caring, and communal. Without exception, behavioral management had been a significant concern in the low SES schools we observed. Like many schools in low SES neighborhoods, these schools had had to deal with fights and other major disruptions. Teachers had spent more time maintaining discipline than teaching, and some classrooms had looked more like holding tanks for misbehavers than schoolrooms. As a result, many parents had routinely applied for transfers for their children to schools in higher socioeconomic neighborhoods.

The principals we observed had worked conscientiously to create a behavioral climate that supported learning. An important element in ensuring that classroom teachers can focus on instruction rather than discipline is character education. Each of the principals we observed had instituted such a program to help their students learn good citizenship, internalize a sense of community, and develop a sense of ownership regarding their school. Among the programs that they implemented were Fred Jones, Responsive Classroom, and Project Wisdom. The specific program was less important than the intended outcomes. Each principal noted, however, programs like these aren't the sole solution to the problem. To supplement the citizenship education program they were implementing, they also invited parents in to work with teachers to present a clearly united front in developing and maintaining a safe and orderly school. In addition, the principals and their vice principals actively supported the teachers when discipline problems occurred, and they were there when difficult conversations needed to be held with parents. In these schools, every child became every staff member's responsibility, and the entire faculty and staff espoused the same behavioral expectations.

The schools we observed instituted a number of other citizenship building initiatives that were successful in achieving student behaviors that supported instruction. Here are a few you might find interesting. One or more of the principals we observed does the following:

- Displays a word (*responsibility, honesty,* and *making choices,* for example) on a sign at the entrance to the building every day, and uses the same word to start morning meetings and refers to it throughout the entire school day.
- Makes a PA system announcement every morning to greet the children, welcome them to school, and share a morning message.
- Undertakes community service projects, such as food drives, packages for soldiers, or leaf raking for the elderly in the neighborhood as school initiatives and encourages students to seek out opportunities to be good citizens and share their deeds with the school newspaper.
- Purchases "message" bracelets that all children put on in the morning with the school name and the motto "Learn-Smart" embossed on it. Every morning the TV sets in every classroom display the message "Put on your bracelets and join the community."
- Installs tuneful chimes in every classroom and areas in which children congregate, and uses the chimes consistently to signal when it's time for children to stop talking and pay attention.
- Sets up peer mediation programs to enable children to learn ways to resolve conflicts without violence.
- Greets every child at the door to the school everyday with a hug, handshake, or high five and a personal message of welcome.

The central and most important purpose of all these and other initiatives is to instill in children a sense of pride and belonging. We can't tell you that a positive change in students' behavior in the buildings we observed was instantaneous, but we can report that within two years these schools experienced a significant turnaround, and education replaced discipline as the focus in every classroom.

COMMUNITY CLIMATE

If your goal is to achieve buy-in from your community, then the community must feel that you're open, welcoming, and *genuine*. The schools we studied featured

- visible principals;
- open classrooms in which parents were invited to share in the educational experiences of their children;
- parents and community members serving on school-improvement planning committees;
- well-placed news articles about the school's achievements; and
- numerous occasions when the neighborhood could come to school and share their cultures, talents, and ideas.

To enhance her visibility and communicate her interest in the community, one of the principals moved her office from an inaccessible back room to a room right next to the front door, so parents coming in could receive a warm hello even if they popped in unexpectedly. It cut down considerably on her private time but was overwhelmingly applauded by the entire school community.

To demonstrate their schools' interest in the community, in many of the schools, teachers were encouraged to call parents routinely with updates about their children or inquire how an "under the weather" student was progressing. Several of the principals sent cards or made congratulatory calls when the siblings of their students experienced a significant success or parents of students had a new baby, bought a new home, or got a promotion. The observable result of this kind of community outreach is that the walls separating these schools from the community became less visible. When parents can see the great things their children are doing, they're more willing to invest their own time and energy in the school's success. When children see that their teachers and parents speak with the same voice and have the same expectations, there are no mixed messages about the importance of getting an education. As we mentioned in Chapter 4, and the schools we observed confirmed, effective parent involvement in their children's education— one of the key factors in successful schools—is more readily forthcoming when we invite, rather than drag, them in.

INSTRUCTIONAL PRACTICES

The ultimate purpose of our schools is, of course, learning. And strong instructional programs were evident in all of the schools we observed.

However, the difference between our schools and schools that are less successful with low SES populations is that in the schools we observed, the instructional programs included the effective strategies and techniques we've discussed in earlier chapters, delivered in a climate conducive to success, with the result that the majority of students regularly demonstrated continuous growth toward benchmarks. Without the existence of the professional, behavioral, and community climates we discussed above, productive instruction doesn't have a healthy environment in which to flourish. If children are worried about their safety, aren't challenged academically, don't have structure, can't take ownership, don't have teachers who know them completely and parents who demonstrate their commitment to education, the soundest instructional practices won't yield successful results.

In the schools we studied, immediate intervention has replaced remediation. The schools are proactive instead of reactive. Continuous formative assessments provide the educational teams with the data necessary to drive instruction based on actual areas of need. The principals and teachers we observed design opportunities for students to receive afterschool instruction, which in many instances anticipates the upcoming curriculum, to build the much needed background knowledge so many low SES children lack. With this model, students are given a jumpstart on the curriculum. In addition, these schools don't wait for summer school to correct problems. They've replaced traditional summer school programs with intervention models that concentrate on providing previews of the upcoming year's curriculum instead of reviews of the past year's failures. All of the teachers we observed found that this extra preparation not only increased students' understanding of the content areas but also improved their self-confidence and, as a result, significantly improved measurable learning and test scores.

Once an atmosphere of trust and collaboration was developed in the entire school community, the doors were open to employing alternative approaches to the standard teaching pedagogy. In these schools, instruction is frequently delivered with alternative methods suited to the learning styles of the students. Among these methods are the use of hands-on manipulatives, discovery learning, and project-based instruction instead of worksheets and lectures. Other innovative approaches used in these schools included the following:

- Postponing the creation of pacing guides until informal assessments were completed to discover the point at which instruction should begin. This was based on the amount of background knowledge acquired by the students in each class. Teachers found that even if they had to back up the starting point to cover gaps in readiness, over the course of the year it didn't prevent them from teaching the entire curriculum. It actually made it less likely they would have to reteach.

- Developing coping programs for the most at-risk students. In one school, three teachers stayed with the same students from first through third grade. They admitted it was a challenge to learn three years of content, but the standardized test results their students achieved at the end of third grade proved to be the best the school had ever seen, with the low SES children scoring as well as, and in some cases better than, their classmates.

- Some of the schools instituted a schoolwide portfolio system. Every child had a math and language arts portfolio and put their best piece of work each week in the portfolio. It was easy for teachers and parents to monitor the amount of growth taking place throughout the year. At the end of the year, teachers were given the portfolios of the students they would be teaching the following year. This gave them a head start in understanding their students' strengths and weaknesses well in advance of the coming year.

How long does it take to turn an education program around like this? The principals we observed reported that within three years of instituting the intervention models, they saw their low SES students achieve on par with their classmates on state-mandated tests.

SUMMARY

The key to creating the school climate and implementing an effective education program for all students, and especially low SES students, is developing the right attitudes in all participants. As you read this chapter, we hope you noticed that formal *programs* aren't part of the process. Even the character education programs that were adopted in the schools we observed were reliant on changing teacher, student, and parent perspectives and beliefs and not on following the programs' rules. One of the teachers in our study said it best: "The most effective development we realized as a staff was that we developed a can-do attitude about all of our children and then showed them the way to succeed. Once they knew that we believed they could, their energy was unstoppable."

Turning poor-achieving schools in low SES neighborhoods into successful centers of learning isn't easy, and it doesn't happen overnight. The successful schools we observed didn't approach the challenge by doing one thing and then another. Their approach was a comprehensive process that focused simultaneously on developing the professional, behavioral, and community climates needed to create a successful education program. As the overall school climate began to change and become embedded with the instructional environment, they were able to implement sound instructional practices successfully.

12 Summary and Conclusions

We want to end this book talking about you, as an education leader. But first, let's briefly revisit what we've presented in the previous 11 chapters. First, we talked about the problem that led us to write this book in the first place—simply stated, the following:

- Nationwide, children of poverty—low SES children—are referred for identification as learning disabled (LD) at a rate that far exceeds the rate for children from higher-income homes.
- There's a lot of statistical evidence that shows that poor classroom performance of low SES children is more likely based on their lack of school-readiness skills than a result of a diagnosed learning disability.
- Standard teaching strategies don't address the problem of low school readiness, with the result that too many teachers and administrators write off low SES children as LD.

We then looked at a study (Howard, 2007) that examined the strategies and techniques used by teachers who work successfully with low SES students. These exemplary teachers of low SES students were selected for the study based on the fact that they had referred no more than one student for LD identification per year over the previous three years, and they had retained no more than one student per year over the same period. Our analyses of the results of that study showed that the common denominator among these teachers was that they all used *four identifiable strategies* and a number of similar techniques to create a learning environment that enabled low SES students to succeed as well as their peers from higher-income homes. The four strategies we discussed are

1. building positive relationships with students and their families;

2. conducting formative and summative assessments;

3. integrating learning experiences; and

4. creating a positive environment for instruction.

As we observed these teachers, we also observed their principals and the school environment, and we identified and discussed other factors that we found to have a significant positive effect on creating equal education opportunities for low SES students. These included

- increasing the involvement of all parents, particularly parents of low SES children;
- developing partnerships with local businesses to increase the resources available to low SES students and parents; and
- developing central office support for programs and strategies to enhance the learning environment for low SES students.

Next, we looked outside of education to discuss effective actions that professionals in other fields take to manage their human resources, and we presented strategies that could be successful for implementing desired changes in the school setting, particularly to support efforts to create education opportunities for low SES students. These included proactive strategies to

- successfully effect change management;
- select the right staff;
- harness the power of organizational and individual competencies to achieve maximum performance; and
- manage faculty and staff performance to achieve your vision.

Finally, we outlined a school-development plan that we believe can effectively guide your efforts in achieving equal education opportunities for low SES students.

BEING THE LEADER IN YOUR SCHOOL

Now, the one critical ingredient needed for the success of the strategies and techniques we've identified is the all-important and essential leadership presence of you! Remember that we've "been there, done that," and one of us is still a building principal. We fully understand the constraints under which you must operate, for example, the expectations of individuals and groups in and outside your school and school district, your "fishbowl" visibility, the pressures of time, and so on. And, we know that every year you're required to take on more and more complicated and demanding issues. To us, however, the singular issue presented in this book—achieving equal education opportunities for low SES students—is an issue that cries out for your intercession. Statistics show that, as a nation, we are failing to fairly serve a growing percentage of our students based on our own *misidentification* of what the problem *really* is and what we *should* be doing to solve it. If you agree, you can do something about it.

We blame much of the failure of schools nationwide to provide equal education opportunities for low SES children on what we call "deficit perception," which manifests itself in statements we hear all the time from teachers and administrators, such as, "These children can't learn," and "These children are unteachable," or worse. Even the national broadcast and print media routinely modify every report of low test scores from "troubled schools" by noting that, of course, the schools are in low-income areas, and it's to be expected. Using the word *these* to describe any part of the population of children and young adults we serve as professional educators is not acceptable under any circumstances. They are "our" kids, not "these" kids, and parents have entrusted them to us as the very best they have to offer. The exemplary teachers and principals we observed have proved over and over again that low SES students can be taught effectively, and they have developed the means to do it. Enough said—let's get back to talking about the importance of you as the education leader in your school and the role we encourage you to assume to ensure equal education opportunities for your low SES students.

MAKING THE MOST OF AN "AMBIGUOUS" SITUATION

Do you have a mind-set that really defines you as an education leader? To find out, find a full-length mirror, stand facing it, spin around in a complete circle three times, and then stamp your right foot on the floor four times. Then boldly announce to yourself, and we stress "yourself," the following statement:

> Look, you hired me to do a job. Now, let me do it, my way, within policy limits of course. Since you're going to hold me totally accountable for how well my students do, let me have the freedom to develop programs and interpret policy in a manner that fits the needs of my school community!

Then believe it yourself.

It's interesting to note that although your authority to do your job is clear—within fixed limits, of course—the "rules" for operating within your authority can be quite ambiguous. And, although ambiguity can be scary for someone who aspires to be a manager, it's the first thing an effective leader looks for. Ambiguity is your opportunity to become more than manager of your building, faculty, and staff and, in fact, be the education leader. It's the loophole that allows you to "be yourself" and to make many of your own decisions. Dunklee (2000) discussed this ambiguity loophole as an opportunity for you to truly lead, not just manage. He noted that

- ambiguity in mandated policy or procedures can lead to some *personal*, on the job *autonomy*;
- although you certainly have limits on your professional behavior, nobody has really set any limits on your *personal* behavior;
- not all situations can be handled by routine, ritualized behavior; and
- managers manage and maintain the status quo, whereas leaders innovate, within limits, and try to meet the needs of individuals. (p. 68, emphasis added)

What does this mean? It simply means that there's a considerable degree of personal discretion built into your school district's administrative structure. Find it, and when you apply it with care, you can initiate and implement strategic changes from *within* your *own* school. You may think you have limited autonomy, but if you dare to take some well-calculated risks and build successful solutions to difficult problems, you'll find that your autonomy, your degree of personal discretion, will skyrocket in the minds and actions of your superiors. We urge you to lead your school and do what needs to be done to maximize the education opportunities for all of your students.

Finally, the climate of your school includes its culture, ecology, cast of characters, and social system. Without *your* personal touch—without your leadership—the positive climate for learning you want to create can't evolve. You can create your school's positive climate, including an innovative and masterfully designed program for low SES students, with the tools you already have available on site. Your forward-looking and effective leadership is the starting point. The climate of success you create should be inviting for all who come to your school to learn, teach, work, or visit.

References

Alexander, K. L., & Entwisle, D. R. (1988). Achievement in the first two years of school: Patterns and processes. *Monographs of the Society for Research on Child Development, 53*(2, Serial No. 218).

Alexander, K. L., Entwisle, D. R., & Thompson, M. S. (1987). School performance, status relations and the structure of sentiment: Bringing the teacher back in. *American Sociological Review, 52*, 665–682.

Algozzine, R., Ysseldyke, J., & McGue, M. (1995). Differentiating low achieving students: Thoughts on setting the record straight. *Learning Disabilities Research and Practice, 10*, 140–144.

Angelo, T., & Cross, K. P. (1993). *Classroom assessment techniques.* San Francisco: Jossey-Bass.

Blair, C., & Scott, K. (2002). Proportion of LD placements associated with low socio-economic status: Evidence for a gradient? *The Journal of Special Education, 36*, 14–22.

Blanchard, K., & Johnson, S. (1982). *The one minute manager.* New York: William Monroe and Company.

Bradley, R. H., & Corwyn, R. F. (1999). Parenting. In L. Balter & C. Tamis-LaMonda (Eds.), *Child psychology: A handbook of contemporary issues* (pp. 339–362). Philadelphia, PA: Psychology Press.

Brown v. Board of Education, 347 U.S. 483 (1954).

Burton, C. B. (1992). Defining family-centered early education: Beliefs of public school, child care and Head Start teachers. *Early Education and Development, 3*, 45–59.

C.A.R.E. Advisory Committee. (2003). *CARE: Strategies for closing the achievement gaps* [Brochure]. Washington, DC: Author.

Carta, J. (1991). Education for young children in inner city classrooms. *American Behavioral Scientist, 4*, 440–453.

Casanova, U. (1996). Parent involvement: A call for prudence. *Educational Researcher, 25*(8), 30–32.

Chambers, J., Parrish, T., & Harr, J. (2002). *What are we spending on special education services in the United States, 1999–2000?* Washington, DC: Special Education Project, Center for Special Education Finance, U.S. Department of Education, Office of Special Education Projects.

Children's Defense Fund. (2006). *2004 Facts on child poverty in America*. Retrieved July 8, 2008, from http://www.chilrensdefense.org/child-research-data-publications/data/children-born-poor-in-2006.html

Child Trends Data Bank. (2007). *Learning disabilities, child trends of national health interview survey data, 1998–2004*. Retrieved March 20, 2009, from www.childtrendsdatabank.org

Cobb, P. (1994). *Theories of mathematical learning and constructivism: A personal view*. Paper presented at the symposium on trends and perspectives in Math Education by the Institute for Mathematics, University of Klazenfurt, Austria.

Corbett, C. (2002). *Effort and excellence in urban classrooms*. New York: Teachers College Press.

Cullingsford, C., & Morrison, M. (1999). Relationships between parents and schools: A case study. *Educational Review, 5*(13), 253–262.

Currie, J., & Neidell, M. (2003). *Getting inside the "black box" of Head Start quality and what matters and what doesn't* (Working Paper 10091). Cambridge, MA: National Bureau of Economic Research.

Dodge, K. A., Pettit, G. S., & Bates, J. E. (1994). Socialization mediators of the relation between socioeconomic status and child conduct problems. *Child Development, 65*, 649–665.

Drame. E. (2002). Sociocultural context effects on teacher's readiness to refer for learning disabilities. *Exceptional Children, 69*, 41–53.

Dunklee, D. R. (2000). *If you want to lead not just manage: A primer for principals*. Thousand Oaks, CA: Corwin.

Dunklee, D. R., & Shoop, R. J. (2006). *The principal's quick reference guide to school law: Reducing liability litigation and other potential legal tangles*. Thousand Oaks, CA: Corwin.

DuPree, M. (1989). *Leadership is an art*. New York: Doubleday.

Education for All Handicapped Children Act of 1975, Pub. L. No. 94-142, 89 Stat.

Education Week. (2004, September 21). Special education. Retrieved March 18, 2009, from http://www.edweek.org/rc//issues/special-education/

Epstein, J. L. (1992). School and family partnerships. In M. Alkin (Ed.), *Encyclopedia of educational research* (pp. 1139–1151). New York: Macmillan.

Feldman, S. (2001, Fall). Closing the achievement gap. *American Educator, 25*(3), 7–9.

Fletcher, J., Shaywitz, S., Shankweiler, D., Katz, L., Liberman, I., & Stuebing, K. (1994). Cognitive profiles of reading disability: Comparisons of discrepancy and low achievement definitions. *Journal of Educational Psychology, 86*, 6–23.

Foster, C. (2000). *Voices for America's children: The progress and the promise*. Baltimore, MD: National Association of Child Advocates.

Fuchs, D., & Fuchs, L. S. (1995). What's "special" about special education? *Phi Delta Kappan, 76*(7), 522–530.

Garmezy, N. (1991). Resiliency and vulnerability to adverse developmental outcomes associated with poverty. *American Behavioral Scientist, 34*, 416–430.

Gershoff, E. (2003). *Low income and the development of America's kindergartners* (Report No. 4, pp. 1–8). New York: National Center for Children in Poverty, Columbia University.

Gerwertz, C. (2007, September 19). High achieving students in low income families said likely to fall behind. *Education Week, 12*.

Gottlieb, J. (1985). Report to the mayor's commission on Committee on the Handicapped practices in New York City. In R. I. Beattie (Ed.), *Special education: A call for quality* (pp. 1–35, App. B). New York: Office of the Mayor.

Gottlieb, J., & Alter, M. (1994). *Evaluation study of the overrepresentation of children of color referred to special education.* Unpublished final report to New York State Education Department, Office of Children With Handicapping Conditions. New York: New York University.

Gottlieb, J., Gottlieb, B. W., & Trongone, S. (1991). Parent and teacher referrals for a psycho-educational evaluation. *Journal of Special Education, 25*, 155–167.

Gottlieb, J., & Weinberg, S. (1999). Comparison of students referred and not referred for special education. *The Elementary School Journal, 99*, 188–199.

Greene, J. P., & Winters, M. A. (2007, Spring). Special education myth: Don't blame private options for rising cost. *Education Next, 7*(2), 67–71.

Gresham, F. (1996). Learning disabilities, low achievement, and mild mental retardation. *Journal of Learning Disabilities, 29*, 570–581.

Grundel, J., Oliveira, M., & Geballe, S. (2003). *All children ready for school: The case for early care and education. A guide for policy makers.* New York: National Center for Children in Poverty.

Haberman, M. (1995). *Star teachers of children in poverty.* Bloomington, IN: Kappa Delta Pi.

Harry, B. (1994). *The disproportionate representation of minorities in special education: Theories and recommendations.* Alexandria, VA: National Association of State Directors of Special Education.

Harvard Public Health. (2007). *American metropolitan areas fail Hispanics and Black children.* Retrieved March 12, 2009, from http://www.hsph.harvard.edu/

Hess, F., & Kendrick, R. (2007, September 25). Too many remedies? *Education Week*, 30–31.

Hill, N. E., & Craft, S. A. (2003). Parent-school involvement and school performance: Mediated pathways among socioeconomically comparable African American and Euro-American families. *Journal of Education Psychology, 91*, 74–83.

Hirsh-Pasek, K., Golinkoff, R. M., & Eyer, D. E. (2003). *Einstein never used flash cards.* Emmaus, PA: Rodale.

Hoffman, L. (2002). Public elementary and secondary students, staff, schools and school districts: School year 2002. *Education Statistics Quarterly, 2002*(356), 1–8. Washington, DC: National Center for Education Statistics.

Howard, L. (2007). *How exemplary teachers educate children of poverty, having low school readiness skills, without referrals to special education.* Unpublished doctoral dissertation, George Mason University, Fairfax, VA.

Kauffman, J. M., Wong, K. L., Lloyd, J., Hung, L., & Pullen, P. L. (1991). What puts pupils at risk: An analysis of classroom teacher's judgments of pupils' behavior. *Remedial and Special Education, 12*, 155–167.

Kavale, K. A. (1995). Setting the record straight on learning disabilities and achievement: The tortuous path of ideology. *Learning Disabilities Research and Practice, 10*, 145–152.

Kavale, K. A., Fuchs, D., & Scruggs, T. E. (1994). Setting the record straight on learning disabilities and low achievement: Implications for policy making. *Learning Disabilities Research and Practice, 9*, 70–77.

Kennedy, P. W., & Dresser, S. G. (2003, February). Creating a competency-based workplace. *Benefits & Compensation Journal, 42*(2), 20–23.

Kennedy, P. W., & Dresser, S. G. (2008, February). *Strategic competencies, basic compensation concepts.* Certificate Series course for the International Foundation of Employee Benefits. Buena Vista, FL.

Kirk, S. A. (1963). Behavioral diagnosis and remediation of learning disabilities. In *Proceedings of the conference on the exploration into the problems of the perceptually handicapped child.* Evanston, IL: Fund for the Perceptually Handicapped Child.

Koonce, D., & Harper, W. (2005). Engaging African-American parents in the schools: A community based consultation model. *Journal of Education and Psychology, 16*(1), 55–74.

Lareau, L. (1994). Parent involvement in schooling: A dissenting view. In C. Fagano & B. Z. Werber (Eds.), *School, family and community interaction: A view from the firing lines* (pp. 61–73). Boulder, CO: Westview Press.

Lee, V., & Burkham, D. (2002). *Inequality at the starting gate.* Washington, DC: Economic Policy Institute.

Lewit, E. M., & Baker, L. S. (1996). Children in special education. *The Future of Children, 6*, 139–51.

Lott, B., (2001). Low-income parents and the pubic schools. *Journal of Social Issues, 57*(2), 247–259.

Machiavelli, N. (1952). *The prince* (L. Ricci, Trans.). New York: The New American Library of World Literature.

Marzano, R. (2004). *Building background knowledge for academic achievement.* Alexandria, VA: Association for Supervision and Curriculum Development.

Maslow, A. H. (1943). A theory of human motivation. *Psychology Review, 50*, 370–96.

McClelland, D. C. (1973). Testing for competence rather than intelligence. *American Psychologist, 28*(1), 1–14.

Myers, H., & Taylor, S. (1998). Family contributions to risk and resilience in African American children. *Journal of Comparative Family Studies, 29*(1), 215–230.

National Association for the Education of Young Children. (1995). *School readiness.* Position statement. Washington, DC: Author.

National Association for the Education of Young Children. (2004). *Where we stand.* Position statement. Washington, DC: Author.

National Center for Children in Poverty. (2004). *Columbia University mailman school of public health.* Retrieved March 13, 2009, from www.nccp.org/pub_lic06b.html

National Center for Education Statistics. (2005). *Number of students exiting special education, by basis of exit and disability* [Excel data file]. Available from Digest of Education Statistics Tables and Figures. Retrieved March 13, 2009, from http://nces.ed.gov/programs/digest/d03/tables/dt109.asp

National Education Goals Panel. (1997). *Special early childhood report.* Washington, DC: U.S. Government Printing Office.

National Education Summit. (1999). *Discussion of schools and standards.* Palisades, NY: National Governor's Association.

National Research Council. (1999). In Bransford, J., Brown, A., Cocking, R., (Eds.), *How people learn: Brain, mind, experience and school* (p. 21). Washington, DC: Washington Academy Press.

Nicholls, J. G. (1979). Development of perception of own attainment and causal attributions for success and failure in reading. *Journal of Educational Psychology, 71*, 94–99.

O'Hara, R. J. (2006). *The social psychology of education: Adults matter.* Retrieved March 13, 2009, from http://collegiateway.org/news/2006-what-it-takes-to-make-a-student

Pardini, P. (2002). The history of special education. *Rethinking Schools Online, 16*(3). Retrieved March 20, 2009, from http://www.rethinkingschools.org/archive/16_03/Hist163.shtml

Pelletier, J. (2005). Design, implementation, and outcomes of a school readiness programs for diverse families. *The School Community Journal, 15*, 89–116.

Pennington, B. F., Gilger, J. W., Olsen, R. K., & DeFries, J. C. (1992). The external validity of age versus IQ-discrepancy definitions of reading disability: Lessons from a twin study. *Journal of Learning Disabilities, 25*, 562–573.

Polakow, V. (1993). *Lives on the edge: Single mothers and their children in the other America.* Chicago: University of Chicago Press.

Ripple, C. H., Gilliam, W. S., Chanana, N., & Zigler, E. (1999). Will fifty cooks spoil the broth? *American Psychologist, 54*, 327–343.

Ritblatt, S. N., Beatty, J. R., Cronan, T. A., & Ochoa, A. M. (2002). Relationships among perceptions of parent involvement, time allocation, and demographic characteristics: Implication for policy formation. *Journal of Community Psychology, 305*(5), 519–549.

Schultze, M., Bremen, J., Crandall, N. F., & Wallace, M. (1994, September). Integrating skills, competencies, and pay. In Chapter 34A, *Compensation Guide* (p. 6). Northbrook, IL: Center for Workforce Effectiveness.

Shonkoff, J., & Phillips, D. (Eds.). (2000). *From neurons to neighborhoods.* Washington, DC: National Academy Press.

Shore, K. (2005, March). Success for ESL students: 12 practical tips to help second language learners. *Scholastic Online.* Retrieved March 20, 2009, from http://www2.scholastic.com/browse/article.jsp?id=4336&FullBreadCrumb=%3C

Sigmon, S. B. (1990). *Critical voices on special education: Problems and progress concerning the mildly handicapped.* Albany: State University of New York Press.

Smith, J., Brooks-Gunn, J., & Klebanov, P. (1997). Consequences of growing up poor for young children. In G. J. Duncan & J. Brooks-Gunn (Eds.), *Consequences of growing up poor* (pp.101–132). New York: Russell Sage.

Stipek, D. (1992). The child at school. In M. Bornstein & M. Lamb (Eds.), *Developmental psychology: An advanced test* (pp. 579–625). Hillsdale, NJ: Erlbaum.

Stipek, D. (1999). Success in school—for a head start in life. In S. S. Luthar, J. A. Burack, D. Cicchetti, & J. R. Wiesz (Eds.), *Developmental psychopathology: Perspectives on adjustment, risk, and disorder* (pp. 75–92). New York: Cambridge University Press.

Tomlinson, C. A. (2004). *Fulfilling the promise of the differentiated classroom.* Alexandria, VA: American Society for Curriculum Development.

U.S. Department of Education. (1997). *Nineteenth annual report to Congress on the implementation of the Individuals with Disabilities Education Act.* Washington, DC: Author. (ERIC Document Reproduction Service No. ED 412 721)

U.S. Department of Education. (2003). *President's commission on excellence in education.* Washington, DC: Author.

U.S. Department of Education. (2008). *Twenty-sixth annual report to Congress on the implementation of the Individuals with Disabilities Education Act.* Washington, DC: Author.

Van Galen, J. (2007, Spring). Late to class: Social class and schooling in the new economy. *Educational Horizon, 85*, 156–167.

Viadero, D. (2007, November 14). No easy answers about NCLB and efforts of "poverty gap." *Education Week,* 12.

Ysseldyke, J., Algozzine, B., Shinn, M., & McGue, K. (1982). Similarities and differences between low achievers and students classified as learning disabled. *The Journal of Special Education, 16*, 73–85.

Zigler, E., & Styfco, S. (1994, February). Head Start: Criticisms in a constructive context. *American Psychologist, 49*(2), 27–132.

CORWIN
A SAGE Company

The Corwin logo—a raven striding across an open book—represents the union of courage and learning. Corwin is committed to improving education for all learners by publishing books and other professional development resources for those serving the field of PreK–12 education. By providing practical, hands-on materials, Corwin continues to carry out the promise of its motto: **"Helping Educators Do Their Work Better."**